Praise for *The 40-Year-Old Vegan*

"Whatever age you are, once you open *The 40-Year-Old Vegan* your health can transform in ways you may not have previously imagined. Author Sandra Sellani writes with a blend of passion and compassion as she shares her culinary vision leading to better health, a better world, and a better life for the animals we share our planet with. I not only enjoyed Sandra's personal insights but also felt a bit like Pavlov's dog upon seeing the Sellani sisters' mouth-watering recipes. I look forward to recommending this book to my patients whether they are forty, fifty, or eighty."

—Carlyn Montes De Oca, author, speaker, and
plant-based nutritional consultant

"*The 40-Year-Old Vegan* is the culmination of Sandra and Susan's lifetime of comfort-food cooking with a vegan twist. Sandra introduced the first Meatless Monday event in the city of Long Beach, California at my restaurant and proved how delicious and accessible vegan food can be."

—Michael Neufeld, restaurant owner, Gaslamp Music + Bar + Kitchen

"The message of *The 40-Year-Old Vegan* is close to my heart. I recognize that all animals feel. I love them and defend them. I know that the meat industry is destroying the world and I know that it is not healthy to eat animal products. That's why I am vegan, because it is the least I can do."

—Ricardo Pimentel Cordero, founder, Tierra de Animales

the 40-Year-Old vegan

75 Recipes to Make You Leaner, Cleaner, and Greener in the Second Half of Life

SANDRA SELLANI AND SUSAN SELLANI

Foreword by JANE VELEZ-MITCHELL

Skyhorse Publishing

Skyhorse Publishing books may be purchased in bulk at special discounts for sales promotion, corporate gifts, fund-raising, or educational purposes. Special editions can also be created to specifications. For details, contact the Special Sales Department, Skyhorse Publishing, 307 West 36th Street, 11th Floor, New York, NY 10018 or info@skyhorsepublishing.com.

Skyhorse® and Skyhorse Publishing® are registered trademarks of Skyhorse Publishing, Inc.®, a Delaware corporation.

Visit our website at www.skyhorsepublishing.com.

10 9 8 7 6 5 4 3 2 1

Library of Congress Cataloging-in-Publication Data is available on file.

Cover design by Jane Sheppard
Cover photography by Sandra Sellani

Print ISBN: 978-1-5107-1850-0
Ebook ISBN: 978-1-5107-1851-7

Printed in China

With love to the women who shared a legacy of love with us through their cooking

Clockwise: Mom (Angie Sellani), Aunt Lena Sellani, Grandma Sellani, Grandma Maira

TABLE OF CONTENTS

FOREWORD

Shakespeare spoke of the seven stages of life. I definitely want to experience every last one. How about you? I'm no Shakespeare but I can certainly testify to the arrogance of youth, that adolescent sense of immortality, where you feel immune to the consequences of drinking, drugging, and binging on fast food. I can also affirm that by your thirties, bravado has given way to distraction. You tell your workaholic self that there's just not enough free time to live mindfully. But, there comes a point when you realize you potentially have less time left on this planet than what you've already lived. You start hearing about friends who've gotten some horrible disease or just look like they're dying. The fear of death seizes you and you finally ask yourself the most important question: *how can I optimize my health to prolong my life and avoid heart disease, cancer, Alzheimer's, or some other devastating fate?*

Good news! This book contains the answer. There is no sacrifice involved. Just a switch in attitude accompanied by a lifestyle change. It's that simple. Do not diet. Diets don't work and studies prove that. Diets require willpower to endure deprivation and you can only do that for so long. This is why most dieters regain their weight and then some.

This book is about abundance, the abundance of a delicious lifestyle that is marked, at its core, by one simple philosophy. Call it a golden rule. Thou shalt not kill. Sound familiar? Despite an endless stream of propaganda to the contrary, you can go through life without killing! Period. The key is to include all sentient beings, like cows, pigs, chickens, turkeys, lambs, and goats on your "no kill" list. Also, please don't steal . . . as in the mother's milk meant to fatten up a calf. Don't kill. Don't steal. That simple framework, when applied to what we consume, eliminates most of the bad food playing field. It seamlessly helps you avoid the minefields of heart disease, cancer, high blood pressure, high cholesterol, obesity, etc.

Think about it. America's leading preventable killer is heart disease. Heart attacks are caused by the obstruction of blood to the heart. The vessels get clogged by plaque. Plaque is caused by cholesterol. Animals produce cholesterol. There is no cholesterol in plants. Simple, right? Unless you are one of the rare individuals with a genetic predisposition to high cholesterol, if you've got too much cholesterol, cut out meat and dairy. Voila!

Now, cancer. The World Health Organization has officially labelled processed meats—which is how most people consume meat—carcinogenic. That's right, look at a chicken nugget or a slice of bacon, and imagine a cigarette.

So, if it's really that simple, if we could really prevent or reverse America's leading killers by switching en masse to a plant-based lifestyle, why wouldn't the best and the brightest be advocating it? Why wouldn't the government be making that happen? Why wouldn't the media be devoting hours of programming to it? The answer is simple: money.

Ever look at the TV commercials? Meat, dairy, pharmaceuticals. These powerful industries not only control the media, they control Congress too. Asparagus doesn't have a lobbyist on K Street, but you can be sure the meat, dairy, and pharmaceutical industries have massive lobbying operations designed to make sure Americans keep buying their products. These industries have enormous sway over US government agencies like the Department of Agriculture, the Interior Department, the Food and Drug Administration, and the National Institutes of Health. Indeed, many have made the case that those taxpayer-funded agencies essentially work for the industries they are supposed to monitor and keep in check.

Big Ag, Big Food, Big Drug: they make money off you on both ends, feeding you the stuff that makes you sick, then treating you with drugs, like cholesterol-lowering pills, when you get fat, sick, and nearly dead. Prevention is not a money maker. "Curing" is. Funny how they never quite come up with that promised "cure" despite a zillion telethons.

There is a ton of money to be made off of keeping you trapped in a Carnist mindset. Carnism is the term coined by Harvard trained social psychologist Dr. Melanie Joy, who describes it as "the invisible belief system that indoctrinates us to eat some animals and love others." To keep you in that mindset, toxic industries spend billions brainwashing you, subliminally associating these self-destructive choices with imagery that insinuates eating hamburgers and milkshakes is somehow patriotic and sexy. Au contraire. You can save a ton of money by kicking the sad standard American diet and switching to a plant-based lifestyle that is better for you, the animals, and the planet.

Think you're an environmentalist? Think again. If you eat meat and dairy, you're a willing participant in an industry that is among the top contributors to climate change, according to UNEP, the United National Environmental Program, and other well-respected institutions. Think about it. It's not just the destruction of the rainforest and other sensitive lands for cattle grazing. It's not just the feces and blood that seeps into our ecosystem. It's the massive amounts of grain, soy, and other feed, plus water, that are required to feed the more than nine billion farm animals slaughtered for food every year in the US alone.

When you switch to a plant-based diet, you can help end world hunger. That's right. If all the food we give billions of farm animals were redirected to starving humans, we could end world hunger today.

Now, for the really good part. Plant-based food is delicious. There are many types of veggies other than corn, carrots, broccoli, and potatoes, although those are tasty too. Brussel sprouts, eggplant, Portobello mushrooms, hearts of palm, kale, and the list goes on and on. Ditto for grains: quinoa, kasha, barley, and my favorite, ancient grains!

Vegan food is an adventure, inspiring us to investigate the recipes of other cultures where veggies are at the center of the plate. But if you're yearning for comfort foods, there are now vegan alternatives for everything from beef, chicken, and fish to cheese and ice cream. Plant-based cuisine is a rapidly growing industry. Virtually every supermarket in America now carries alternatives to cruel, unhealthy choices.

So, switch that attitude and join us. We're a fun lot. It's a great feeling knowing you're going to get through the day without hurting an innocent animal by eating food that's lower in calories, and has zero cholesterol. Oh, and there are plenty of veggies and grains with protein, like kale and quinoa, to name two. There's nothing more enjoyable than a meal that is guilt free and cruelty free. Join our movement by using the Happy Cow app. Seek out the vegan restaurants and meetups popping up around the world. When you're in the compassion crowd, you'll always find a party with a peaceful plate. Bon Appetit!

Jane Velez-Mitchell
Founder/editor of JaneUnChained.com

INTRODUCTION

"Don't mind if I fall apart. There's more room in a broken heart."
—Carly Simon, "I Believe in Love"

Why write a book on plant-based living for people over the age of forty? Shouldn't the phrase "You can't teach an old dog new tricks" apply? Well, if you think forty is old, it might apply, but as you've likely learned, forty is far from old. I'm well past forty, and still don't feel "my age." I fought the aging process every step of the way, kicking and screaming, only to discover something deeply beautiful about getting older. Something I couldn't have known until I arrived. Something I hope you will also learn from reading this book. It has a lot to do with Carly Simon's beautiful words.

Falling Apart or Coming Together?

If you're forty years of age or older, you've likely taken a hit somewhere along the way. You've lost a job. Agonized through a divorce. Been a caretaker for an elderly family member while raising growing children. Looked at a dwindling checking account, wondering how you're going to have enough money to pay for groceries, let alone the thirty-year mortgage staring you smack in the face. You've gone to a funeral or two. You've had your heart broken into a million pieces. *Thank goodness.* These hardships force us to lose the arrogance and invincibility of our youth and open ourselves up to the idea—and the exciting possibility—that maybe we still have something left to learn.

But the beauty of being broken by life, if we do not allow our hardships to make us bitter, is that each painful break expands our heart's capacity for love, for ourselves, and for others. We might be more open to change now than we were in the past. A relationship gone wrong could spark the idea that perhaps we can live life without a partner, but not without a purpose. A health scare might make us more open to getting out into nature for daily walks, or changing our diet. The loss of a loved one can help us realize we must say "I love you" more openly and frequently to those who remain. We have come to know and accept our weaknesses and our strengths. We've pondered our mortality. We've softened a little, in a good way. The cracks that surface because of life's shifting landscape can expose a beautiful vulnerability and willingness to change. We've learned empathy because we've been on the receiving end of someone else's kindness. We've allowed ourselves to depend on someone without seeing it as a sign of weakness. We've come to understand love in its many forms. I ask that you open your mind and heart as you read the pages ahead. If you let it, this book can transform your life. It might even save it.

Food, Love, and Life: The Bigger Picture

This is not a diet book, although practicing its principles can help you lose weight and keep it off for good. This book is not intended to "convert" you to being vegan, although if you read on you might be more inclined to consider veganism as a path to what has previously eluded you in your weight and health goals. This book is not about blaming or shaming anyone for their food choices. This book explains one path to a new way of life that many are discovering is simple in its execution and profound in its rewards. This book is about rebuilding our health and our lives in beautiful, meaningful, and sustainable

ways. The cracks our bodies and our lives have endured have allowed a greater capacity for love. The cracks, after all, are where the light shines in.

I was compelled to write this book with my twin sister, Susan, who is not a vegan but eats a predominantly plant-based diet, to underscore the fact that veganism is often a process, and that moving in the direction of veganism should be considered a healthy and celebratory step in the right direction. My sister was instrumental in helping me recreate the recipes of our youth into healthier, vegan versions and showing others how to do the same. We don't want anyone to feel judged by their food choices, but we do want our readers to feel encouraged to take steps in the direction of veganism and to know of the benefits of a plant-based lifestyle.

Many people in my life have shared their knowledge of plant-based living, and continue to do so. I want to continue that tradition of sharing. I've learned much from my long journey to veganism, which started more than thirty years ago, to my culinary training, and to my realization that the only thing that will sustain us as we grow older is our ability to find joy in things large and small; vegan living is rooted in joy, kindness, and peace. It's been said that in order to be happy, one must have something to look forward to. That's often a difficult concept when, by this age, many of us have already experienced what we consider to be life's most successful milestones: marriage, a career, a home, an education, children. Is there really something left to experience? Can the best years of our lives still be ahead of us? They can be if we learn to find meaning and joy in simple things. In fact, we can find them in what may seem like the most unlikely of places—our dinner plates.

One of the easiest and most profound ways to find joy happens three times a day with what we put on our plates and in our bodies. You may not see the connection now, but there is a profound joy to vegan living that isn't discussed nearly enough, a joy in knowing you have cared enough for the vulnerable creatures of this earth to allow them to have their own path, just as you have yours.

Susan and I have always enjoyed sharing what we love with others, whether it be new products or old recipes. Growing up in an Italian family, food was always a cultural expression of love and celebration, and through our lives we have enjoyed making our favorite meals for friends and family. Veganism extends the realm of love beyond friends and family to include animals and the earth we inhabit with them.

Susan and I look forward to sharing recipes handed down to us from our mother, aunt, and Italian grandmothers, as well as newer recipes inspired by my residence in and Susan's visits to Southern California. You'll also read inspirational stories from some other "40-year-old vegans" who have turned to plant-based living in the second half of life. Their stories will hopefully shatter any myths or stereotypes you might have about vegans. Are they hippie radicals trying to convert the world? No, they're just people who have found a way of life that has forever changed them, demonstrating that simple choices can result in profound transformations. This transformative element is something many people don't expect when they start eating this way; it's just a beautiful by-product. Finally, you will come to know that you can exercise the profound power of kindness to change your life and the world by something as simple as the food choices you make.

Where is Love? A Greater World Problem

It seems that with each passing year, we witness a greater absence of love than ever before. Bullying is ubiquitous. If you have children, you've seen it in their schools and online. But bullying doesn't begin and end in the playground or on social media sites. We see bullying in the workplace. We see politicians, businessmen, coworkers, and adults in general behaving badly. But there's more. There's another type of victimization and violence we don't see because it is carefully and intentionally kept away from us. Or maybe we're aware of it but we don't want to acknowledge its presence. Whether we choose to acknowledge it or not, there are unspeakable atrocities that happen to millions of kind and gentle animals worldwide on a daily basis. Is it possible that there's a connection between the unbridled rage we see in our world and the decisions we are making at the most basic level—our food choices? Why is there so much rage in our world? Why is unkindness so pervasive? Shouldn't we know better by now?

For those of you who are compelled to live a kinder life, regardless of how you choose to eat, I encourage you to read on and see that everything we do is connected. Our food, our planet, our behavior, our health; these elements bring value and meaning to our lives. This book provides just one element, but it's an important step in finding your path to peace because it's tenets are so basic, profound, and attainable. How easy is it, after all, to begin a path that starts with comforting, nutritious food that's good for you, your family, and the planet? How easy is it to know that you're not alone in wanting to live a better life and create a better, more peaceful planet for your children or future generations? If you are reading this book, you are part of a growing number of people who are finding the joy of eating and living in a whole new way that doesn't involve counting calories or being a nutrition expert; a way that involves bringing our hearts and souls into the process of eating by fully understanding the consequences of our eating habits and choices. Don't be afraid of what you might have to give up by eating in this new way. You will gain exponentially more.

Take it Easy

The difference between this book and every other vegan book available is that I'm going to make it as easy as possible for you to transform your health, your life, and the world and to connect the dots between food choice and the joy and connectivity you can experience in your daily life—especially to people over the age of forty. I became a vegetarian at age twenty-five, but the full benefits of my plant-based lifestyle didn't become apparent to me until

I became a vegan at age fifty. And while my sister Susan is not vegan, she chooses to eat a mostly plant-based diet, and has lost weight and lowered her cholesterol in doing so, demonstrating that one small change in the direction of veganism can make significant changes in your life.

You've likely talked to people who felt better after changing or eliminating just one component from their diets, like milk or red meat. It was a small step that made a big difference for them. Imagine the difference a few more changes can make for them and for you. It's important to acknowledge the importance of the transition period itself and the types of food that can help you seamlessly move from your current dietary practices to a healthy life without struggling with the hunger and frustration of fad diets. Even if you never become 100 percent vegan, the closer you move to the plant-based end of the spectrum, the more health benefits you will reap.

Your path toward veganism can take a day, a month, or a year—you decide. After all, if you are over forty you *can* still learn new tricks. But you must first be convinced that the new tricks will serve you better than the old ones. And when you do, you will realize that life begins, not at forty, but when your values and lifestyle choices are in full alignment. If you believe kindness is a virtue, this book is for you. What you may not know is that when you incorporate kindness into every choice, including your food choices, your body, your life, and your planet will be forever transformed.

Sandra Sellani
The 57-Year-Old Vegan

PART I

Sandra (left) and Susan (right) in the early sixties,
being very fashion forward with their baby "faux" hawks

Sandra (left) and Susan (right) in the mid-sixties as
flower girls in their Aunt Teresa and Uncle John's wedding

Sandra (left) and Susan (right), age 38, at their
20-year high school reunion

Sandra (left) and Susan (right) celebrating their
55th birthday in beautiful Venice Beach, California

CHAPTER 1

A Tale of Two Sisters

"There is no spectacle on earth more appealing than that of a beautiful woman in the act of cooking dinner for someone she loves."
—Thomas Wolfe

Susan and I grew up in an Italian household in Northeastern Pennsylvania, watching our mother Angie, our Aunt Lena, Grandma Sellani, and Grandma Maira make countless authentic Italian meals from scratch. We learned to cook at an early age, and meat and dairy were always a part of our daily meals. It wasn't until I moved to Napa, California as part of a school internship at the age of twenty-two that everything changed. I met a friend, Bobbie Theodore (who is still a friend to this day), who introduced me to a vegetarian lifestyle.

Bobbie was a vegetarian, and I was curious about this way of eating, so she started explaining the reasons behind her diet, which were rooted in animal advocacy and the desire to abstain from any practice that involved animal cruelty. I had always loved animals, yet never made the connection between the food I ate and the cruel practices that were part of factory farming. I confessed to Bobbie,

I wasn't sure if I could give up meat because it was so much a part of my Italian heritage. Then Bobbie said something I never forgot. She said, "It's better to give it up for one meal a week, than not at all." At that moment, I realized this was something I could do. I was so touched by the fact that Bobbie didn't blame me or others for eating meat, that the conversation stayed with me. I didn't make changes right away. Old habits die hard. But I ultimately did become vegetarian a few years later at age twenty-five. Susan, while not vegan, eats less meat and dairy than she has in the past. She stays slim and has reduced the high cholesterol that plagues our family without the use of medication, simply by adding more veggies to her diet and cutting back on meat and dairy. Both Susan and I love the recipes from our childhood, and in this book, we will share our updated, healthier vegan versions with you.

This book combines three concepts to help you go vegan in the second half of life:

The acknowledgement that if you are over forty, a transition to veganism may not happen overnight, but it can happen, and the process is delicious and fun. Your current food choices are made up of your history, your heritage, and your habits. But we will make a compelling argument that vegan living, or taking steps toward vegan living, can have a significant and positive impact on your life. We're here to help you lean in to veganism and benefit from each step along the way.

The spirit of inclusion to all readers. Whether you are a vegan or an omnivore, we are not here to judge. We are here to demonstrate a way of living that we think will add health and joy to your life. Even if you never become 100 percent vegan, we think the changes you make will be so inspirational that you'll want to keep going. How many "diets" allow you to go at a pace that you dictate?

Vegan food is comfort food! Susan and I are true foodies—we wouldn't promote any recipes unless they were absolutely delicious. These recipes aren't just good vegan recipes; they are delicious recipes that anyone will enjoy. They have been vegan tested and omnivore approved; many are vegan versions of the food our mother and grandmothers taught us to make many years ago in our home state of Pennsylvania. Some are newly inspired recipes that Susan and I have come to enjoy after my move to California and her many visits here, starting in the early eighties.

My Switch to Veganism

A few years after meeting Bobbie, I watched a documentary based on the book *Animal Liberation* by Peter Singer. While I knew there were cruel practices taking place against animals, I couldn't have imagined what I saw in the documentary. Knowing that animals suffer is not the same as seeing actual footage of it because the average person cannot even comprehend the level of horror that takes place on factory farms. It's not even within our frame of reference. I decided at that moment to go vegetarian. I gave up fish the first week, chicken the second week, then beef, pork, and all remaining animal flesh the third week. I stayed a vegetarian from age twenty-five to fifty. And, yes, there were times during those twenty-five years when I slipped up and ate meat and felt guilty, but that's all part of the process. Know that habits take time to break, and learn from mistakes, rather than allow them to derail you. Eventually, I lost all cravings for meat and dairy.

At age fifty, while training for the New York Marathon, I was following a vegetarian diet plan that was part of a ninety-day home workout program called P90X[1]. I noticed that in the third month of the program, the diet plan was essentially vegan, so I stayed with it. I also noticed that after going vegan, I no longer had symptoms of ulcerative colitis, a condition that plagued me since the age of twenty-two. At age fifty-three I attended vegan culinary school at Matthew Kenney Culinary Academy in Los Angeles, California. I was more inspired than ever to keep a vegan lifestyle, but still craved the comfort foods of my childhood. That's where twin sister Susan comes in.

"Veganizing" Recipes

Recipes were rarely written down in the Sellani household. Susan, however, has an amazing memory. When I prepare vegan renditions of our childhood favorites, it is Susan who recalls the original recipes, not just the ingredients, but the process of how they were prepared. While we live on separate coasts, we spend many hours on the phone discussing our favorite recipes. (Many are between fifty and one hundred years old!)

As I mentioned earlier, Susan is not a vegan. She is what I call a VIP (Vegan in Progress) who eats little meat and dairy and enjoys a lot of salads, pastas, quinoa, and other plant-based dishes. She has kept thin by reducing meat and dairy from her diet and adding a significant amount of fruits and vegetables. This is an important piece of information because this book was not intended for vegan readers only—quite the contrary. It was intended to help anyone in the second half of life make a transition to vegan eating for health benefits, weight loss, and benefits to the planet. You will find that you can lose weight simply by reducing the meat and dairy in your diet while adding lots of colorful fruits and vegetables. While this book is intended for anyone to enjoy, all recipes are completely vegan with no animal products, not even honey.

Becoming a vegan does not always happen overnight. What's most important is knowing that every effort toward a plant-based lifestyle makes a difference. And if you're over forty, there's never been a better time to go vegan.

[1] https://www.beachbody.com/product/fitness_programs/p90x.do?code=SEMB_P90X_GOOGLE&utm_campaign=Google_Brand_P90X_Alpha&utm_term=p90x&trackingid=sdOlhkImk&gclid=Cj0KEQiA6bq2BRC6ppf0_83Z1YIBEiQAgPYNvX9lcw1VWBhoKFw4MCnLjNT-DhZ28ZpH0drW6GZz0hRUaAp868P8HAQ

CHAPTER 2

Why Vegan? Why Now?

"Within two weeks of switching to a plant-based diet, IGF-1 levels in the bloodstream drop sufficiently to help slow the growth of cancer cells."
—Kathy Freston, Huffington Post

As I stated earlier, being over the age of forty can open our minds and hearts to new ideas. Experiencing vulnerability helps us realize that maybe we can still learn and experience new things. You might find yourself saying that you want to make changes at this time of your life.

Who is the 40-Year-Old Vegan?

If you are making an effort to eat more plant-based foods in the second-half of life, then *you* are the 40-year-old vegan. This is about the *transition* from being an omnivore to being a vegan as much as it is about being completely vegan. It's important to note, again, that I am vegan while Susan still eats some animal products, although much less than she did years ago. Very often veganism involves a transition, and it's important to acknowledge where Susan and I are in the process. We both started out as meat and dairy eaters, and it's not always realistic for some people to

make a drastic change from their current diet to veganism. Some books have an all or nothing approach, and while it is my hope that you are inspired to become vegan after reading this book, I realize that your end result might end up bringing you closer to veganism than you are now, and that's a good thing. Even if you never become 100 percent vegan, but eliminate some of the saturated animal fat products from your diet, you would already be doing something good for yourself and the planet.

This book is about making some easy revisions in your life that will help you enjoy the foods you've always loved with a little bit of a twist. It's not as crazy or drastic as you think because we know that making changes in the second half of life can be a little challenging. The tummy wants what the tummy wants and we know it's hard to make changes unless they're gradual and enjoyable. Those changes might include statements listed below in the 40YOV Quiz.

THE 40YOV QUIZ

The following quiz will tell you how this book will help you achieve your health, diet, and lifestyle goals. After each item, give yourself a score of "1" (does not apply to me at all) to "5" (completely applies to me). Calculate your total score by adding the number you assigned to each statement.

1. I want to reduce, eliminate, or reverse disease as much as possible with diet and as little as possible with medication. _____

2. I want to reduce mid-life weight gain. _____

3. I want to feel more energetic. _____

4. I want to improve my regularity. _____

5. I want to find new ways to simplify my life. _____

6. I want to find new ways to make kindness a daily practice. _____

7. I want to prepare healthier meals for my family. _____

8. I want to eliminate cholesterol from my diet. _____

9. I want to leave a better planet for future generations. _____

10. I want more restful sleep at night. _____

11. I no longer have the luxury of eating unhealthy foods because of my current health condition(s). _____

12. I want more opportunities to practice joy and spirituality in simple, daily acts. _____

Total Score: _____

What Does Your Score Mean?

48–60 points: You're Going to **Love** This Way of Life

It will have a profound impact on your health and well-being. It's not just about eating the right foods, but about eating foods that make you feel right—with your health and your world view. You see food as more than just fuel. It holds an important meaning for you, socially, traditionally, spiritually, or culturally. This diet will help you feel that all parts of your life are in alignment.

36–47 points: A Change Will Do You Good

A vegan diet makes sense for you, either for health reasons or simply for adjusting to a new phase of life where simple, healthy choices will improve your quality of life now and in the future. You enjoy good food and want to make smart decisions to maintain your health or stave off health issues in the years ahead due to aging or bad dietary habits.

35 or Below: Baby Steps

You might find that eating vegan one to two days a week is a great starting point. You may not have the significant health issues, aging issues, or motivation to make big changes right now, but can definitely benefit from the little ones now and in the future. You might be surprised that once you take baby steps,

you're going to feel good enough to make a quantum leap.

A Closer Look at Your Score

Look at the areas of the test where you gave yourself higher scores. The information below will go into more detail about why these areas can have an impact on your life.

1. I want to reduce, eliminate, or reverse disease as much as possible with diet and as little as possible with medication

Think a vegan diet is an extreme way to stay healthy? Consider this: *The Journal of the America Medical Association* (JAMA) reported that physician error, medication error, and adverse events from drugs or surgery kill 225,400 people each year. In other words, these products of our health care system are the third leading cause of death in the US behind cancer and heart disease.[2] Suddenly, eating plants doesn't sound as extreme or scary as the alternative—the adverse effects of dealing with an overburdened healthcare system.

A vegan diet has been associated with the prevention, elimination, or even reversal of cancer, heart disease, Type 2

[2]Campbell, T. Colin, & Campbell, Thomas M., *The China Study: The Most Comprehensive Study of Nutrition Ever conducted and The Startling Implications or Diet, Weight Loss and Long-term Health*, p. 15.

diabetes, stroke, macular degeneration, migraines, erectile dysfunction, and arthritis, to name just a few. How many prescriptions do you need to ease any number of these health conditions, some of which are related to diet, lack of exercise, or poor lifestyle choices? Which medications have the potential for side effects or drug interactions?

Medication is often a necessary path to healing, and food is often a preventative measure. But what if you could eat the right foods to avoid certain medications? What if you could eliminate some of the prescriptions in your medicine cabinet? Many people have done just that on a vegan diet; I'm one of them. In my early life, poor eating habits combined with stress led to serious illness and the need for medication. Making better food choices led to the elimination of four prescriptions for me. I'll share more on that later. That doesn't mean vegans will never experience health issues and never have to take medication. We are all products of our genetic makeup and predisposed to certain illnesses. We are also exposed to chemicals, carcinogens, stress, and injuries in our daily lives. But when we look at the things we can control, food is one of the easiest and most enjoyable changes we can make, with incredible health benefits.

2. I want to reduce mid-life weight gain

No one loves love handles, but chances are, if you're over forty, you just need to look down at your waist to find them. Even people who have been thin their entire lives can find a "pooch" appearing in their midsection and wonder how this could happen to them.

Eating a whole food plant-based diet can help you battle the bulge. This doesn't mean becoming a junk food vegan and living on French fries. It means stocking up on fresh produce, beans, and whole grains. It means keeping fats, even healthy fats like avocado and olive oil, to lower levels and avoiding the seduction of highly processed foods whenever possible.

Most vegans I know don't count calories. They become more in tune with their bodies, eating only when hungry, and stopping when full. They make healthy choices a habit, so even if they overdo it a little, it's not going to have a negative impact. By eating the right foods mindfully, the spare tire will recede, the scale will become your friend, and you'll realize that Mother Nature always provides what we need. As it is often said in the vegan community, eat plants, not something that is made in a plant.

3. I want to feel more energetic

Who doesn't get occasionally tired after age forty? You're working, you're raising a family, and maybe you're taking classes or volunteering. When you drop weight, you feel more energetic. When you fuel your body with fruits, veggies, and grains, you will have sustained energy. It sounds too simple to be true, but it really isn't. Yes, you will have to train yourself to appreciate the flavor of fresh foods again. If you're used to a diet of greasy fast food, high fat, high sugar, high processed meals, you will need to detox. When you do, you'll start to realize that a spoon full of almond butter on an apple slice tastes divine. You'll appreciate a soft, sweet pear, or fresh spinach sautéed with a little olive oil and garlic. A flatter tummy will appear and energy will return. It's a great feeling and it doesn't have to go away with age. This books includes several stories by individuals who became vegan after the age of forty, and a common denominator among them is the energy they felt as a result of their dietary changes. If you can't go cold turkey to a plant-based diet, simply start incorporating more fruits and veggies into your meal, leaving less room on your plate for meat and dairy. You'll start to feel the difference.

4. I want to improve my regularity

Remember when you were #1 at going #2? Good times. But most people don't get the daily fiber necessary to keep them healthy. It is recommended that we get 14 grams of fiber for every 1,000 calories consumed. So a 2,000 calorie a day diet means 28 grams of fiber.[3] On the Standard American Diet of meat, dairy and processed foods, that's not always easy. On a vegan diet, it's a cinch. Lack of fiber can lead to chronic constipation that can lead to hemorrhoids and diverticulitis. Why risk any of this when it's so easy to get your fiber from delicious foods? Add a cup of garbanzo beans to your salad, have a sweet potato as a snack, enjoy a morning smoothie with bananas, blueberries, and raspberries and you have easily increased your fiber intake. The fiber not only helps with regularity but also keeps you feeling full, which leads to less snacking and more weight loss. Below is just a partial list of vegan fiber sources.[4]

Food	Grams of Fiber
1 Brussels Sprout	.5
½ cup brown rice	1.8
1 tbsp. ground flax seeds	1.9
½ cup carrots	2.3
1 cup broccoli	2.4

[3]http://www.vegetariantimes.com/article/ask-the-nutritionist-how-much-fiber-do-i-really-need/
[4]http://www.huffingtonpost.ca/2013/10/31/high-fibre-foods_n_4178239.html

Food	Grams of Fiber
½ cup red lentils	4.0
1 medium-sized apple	4.4
1 cup quinoa	5.2
1 medium-sized pear	5.5
1 (9 in) cooked parsnip	5.8
1 bunch spinach	7.5
1 oz. chia seeds	10.6
1 cup black beans	15.0
1 cup white beans	18.6

5. I want to simplify my life

Have you noticed that as you get older, simplicity beckons you like an old friend? Maybe it's a longing for the effortless days of childhood. Maybe it's a realization that time is precious and fleeting, so you want to be efficient in how you use yours. I notice that I don't socialize as much in my fifties. I enjoy the company of friends, but simply need more alone time. I also don't desire as many material things as I once did; I have far fewer items of clothing, shoes, and jewelry. It's the same with food. Vegan food is simple food. I know there are a lot of trendy vegan restaurants out there that complicate things. They'll serve you a meal that consists of a big white plate with an artfully placed kidney bean and a marigold petal in the middle, then charge you $50, but that's not what I believe vegan food is all about.

For me, it's about ample portions of healthy, fresh food. It's about shopping more frequently at a farmers' market or at your grocer's produce aisle and appreciating the beautiful bounties of each season: yellow summer squash, autumn red pears, fleshy pink watermelons, deep green kale, ruby red grapefruits, crimson colored apples, bright orange mangoes. When I bite into a mango, I'm in heaven. Avocado is my idea of decadence. Find out which foods speak to you and build a meal around them, remember that "meals" don't always mean cooking. A fresh fruit salad with a sprinkle of nutmeg is an amazing way to start the day. A bowl of fresh heirloom tomatoes, red onion, and basil leaves drizzled with balsamic vinegar and paired with a crusty piece of whole grain bread is so satisfying. And so simple.

6. I want to make kindness a daily practice

Something about getting older and closer to our inevitable mortality makes us put things in perspective and reminds us of the importance of being a kinder, gentler person. Every day on TV you witness every level of cruelty from cyberbullying to school shootings. You've witnessed rude behavior in the workplace. You find yourself saying *what is wrong with people*? It's hard to understand what drives people to do such cruel and unimaginable things, but we also have to look at what contributions we are making to the world, both kind and cruel. Kindness begins at home and it begins on our plate—if we allow it to.

I won't lecture about the inhumane torture that animals endure for the production of meat and dairy, but if you saw footage of it you would be horrified. I encourage you to go online and look up "factory farming" on YouTube. You'll see everything you need to see in about five minutes. I know it's hard to deny yourself the meat and dairy you've enjoyed for an entire lifetime. I grew up in an Italian family eating meatballs, and pork, and cheese. I get it. If you can't give it up altogether, at least go one day a week without meat. It makes a huge difference. For example, if you were vegan just one day a week, fifty-two days a year, you would save approximately thirty-two animals from being killed. You might say you don't care about animals raised for food but you would never torture or mutilate your family dog or cat, so why is it okay to do so to any other animal that is capable of feeling pain? The TV commercials you see about "happy cows" are simply not true. The new surge of "humanely raised" livestock is a marketing ploy. There is no such thing as humane killing unless the animals are anesthetized prior to being slaughtered, and I can assure you that's not happening. With pressure from animal advocacy groups, many factory farms are finding ways to be less cruel to animals, but these practices simply reduce cruelty, they do not eliminate it.

Practicing veganism means going to bed at night with a clear conscience, knowing that you did not cause another creature's pain, and that's a great feeling. Vegetariancalculator.com shows the impact of eating vegan on animals and the planet. When you can see the numbers, you will realize you can make a difference.

7. I want to prepare healthier meals for my family

Many people at the age of forty find themselves in-between two generations, caring for both children and elderly parents. If you are cooking for your family, you have a profound influence on others. Think about your own eating habits and how heavily they were influenced by what was served in your own household when you were a child. If your parents ate healthy food, chances are you did too. Preparing healthy food for your family can keep them from being part of the growing number of individuals with health issues such as obesity, diabetes, and heart disease. Teaching your family how to eat healthy meals is one of the greatest gifts you can give them. Later in this book, you will read stories of people who became vegan after age forty, and in doing so, helped their family members significantly improve their health in the process.

8. I want to eliminate cholesterol from my diet

High cholesterol comes from two sources. First, it is genetic. You might have been unlucky enough to inherit it. Susan and I did. But there's hope—the second source of cholesterol is animal products; meat and dairy. A plant-based diet contains no cholesterol—not even foods with fat like avocado, olive oil, and nuts. So, while you can't always change what is happening to you genetically, you can at least control the cholesterol you put into your body. In other words, your genes don't have to be a death sentence. Your diet can shape your destiny.

9. I want to leave a better planet for future generations

If you've ever seen cities torn apart by riots, where the residents looted and burned down buildings in their own neighborhoods, you may have asked *why would someone destroy their own community?* And yet, we all do this to our earth every day for the same reason as the rioters. We act in the moment without considering the consequences of our behavior. Consider these statistics from One Green Planet[5]:

- More than 37 percent of methane emissions are the result of factory farming. Methane's global warming potential is twenty times that of carbon dioxide.
- More than 260 million acres in the US alone have been cleared for crop fields, the majority of those crops grown exclusively to feed livestock, not people.
- 70 percent of the earth's fresh water supply goes to industrial agriculture, not people.
- The run from agriculture pollutes our water supply and can destroy entire ecosystems with toxicity and lethality to both humans and animals.

At first, it might not seem terrible that crops and water are used for livestock that will eventually feed people, but it's important to note that the food and water used to feed

[5]http://www.onegreenplanet.org/animalsandnature/factory-farming-is-killing-the-environment/

the animals would feed more people than the animals will feed once slaughtered. For example, according to FoodTank, an organization focused on sustainable ways to feed the earth's 7 billion people, it takes approximately:

- 1,799 gallons of water to produce 1 pound of beef
- 216 gallons to produce 1 pound of soybeans
- 108 gallons to produce 1 pound of corn

To take the example further, Extension.org, an organization that focuses on climate and food systems, tells us it takes about 4.67 pounds of corn to produce a pound of beef.[6] We could feed more people on five pounds of corn than one pound of beef. Some will argue that the beef has protein, but Americans have been convinced that we need more protein than we actually do. Advertising and the meat and dairy industry want you to believe that you need to overload yourself with animal protein to be healthy and strong. According to T. Colin Campbell, MD, author of *The China Study: The Most Comprehensive Study of Nutrition Ever Conducted and the Startling Implications for Diet, Weight Loss, and Long-term Health* our ideal diet should consist of 80 percent carbohydrates, 10 percent fat, and 10 percent protein—all plant-based[7]. Dr. Caldwell B. Esselstyn, Jr., MD, author of *Prevent & Reverse Heart Disease,* adds "The protein available in a diet of whole grains, legumes, fruit and beans, and red, yellow, and green vegetables is adequate to nourish even professional champion athletes such as those who compete in the iron man races, professional football, mixed martial arts, and track and field. Avoid protein drinks. The extra protein is truly unnecessary and has the potential for harm if it contains animal protein."[8]

That is why, when people ask me if vegans like animals more than people, I explain to them that when we take care of animals, we DO take care of people! We take care of their health; we make more food and water available to people worldwide; we prevent or reduce diseases; we cultivate an atmosphere of gratitude and kindness. Animal advocacy has a direct and positive impact on human health, longevity, and economic well-being.

The meat and dairy industries are simply not a sustainable means of feeding

[6]http://articles.extension.org/pages/35850/on-average-how-many-pounds-of-corn-make-one-pound-of-beef-assuming-an-all-grain-diet-from-background

[7]https://www.goodreads.com/work/quotes/19174391-whole-rethinking-the-science-of-nutrition

[8]http://www.dresselstyn.com/site/books/prevent-reverse/about-the-book/

our planet. We can be proactive and start a plant-based lifestyle now, or be forced into it as we continue to devour scarce resources. We talk about saving the planet. We recycle and drive fuel-efficient cars. We don't litter. These are all important gestures. But plant-based living can help you make significant, daily contributions to the planet. Consider this. Each *day* you eat a vegan diet you save[9]:

- 1,100 gallons of water
- 45 pounds of grain
- 30 square feet of forested land
- 20 pounds of CO2 equivalent
- 1 animal's life

Imagine the resources we would save if everyone went vegan for just one day, and you'll start to see how far-reaching the impact of this diet can be.

10. I want more restful sleep at night

If you've noticed that it's harder to get a good night's sleep after age forty, you're not alone. Studies show that one in three Americans are sleep deprived; if you are among them, you know that sleep deprivation can cause distress, depression, and impairment of your daily functioning. Insufficient sleep is also linked to obesity,

high blood pressure, and even Alzheimer's Disease.[10]

Dr. Neal Barnard of the Physician's Committee for Responsible Medicine dispels the myth that protein is needed to help sleeping. In fact, he states that "complex carbohydrates stimulate the release of serotonin—a neurotransmitter that calms your brain and helps you sleep." In addition to reducing alcohol and caffeine, exercising, and keeping a regular schedule, he recommends "building your dinner around starchy foods, like pasta, rice, and potatoes" to help you fall asleep and stay asleep. So having a dish of pasta for dinner will help you sleep—but if you add chicken, meatballs, or other animal proteins, it will undo the effects of the carbohydrates. Additionally, if you wake up in the middle of the night and can't get back to sleep, he suggests eating two slices of bread. Again, the carbs will aid you in getting back to sleep. It turns out that pasta and bread are just what the doctor ordered.

So if you're one of many people who think that carbs are the enemy, you can rejoice in knowing that they are absolutely essential for our well-being and you will

[9]http://www.rosenlake.net/cowspiracy.html

[10]http://www.pcrm.org/nbBlog/eat-your-way-to-a-good-nights-sleep

see plenty of carb-rich recipes in this book. You're welcome.

11. I no longer have the luxury of eating unhealthy foods because of my current health conditions

Some people eat vegan to stave off future health problems. But if you're among those people who already have health issues that require dietary changes, you know that it's never enjoyable to be told you have to suddenly "give up" the foods you love.

Regardless of your health condition, it is likely it would improve by abstaining from high fat, high salt, high cholesterol, high sugar, or highly processed foods. And while you should consult your physician with any changes to your diet, most doctors will agree that adding fruits, vegetables, and whole grains to your diet is significantly helpful.

12. I want to practice joy and spirituality in simple, daily acts

How many times do you rush through meals, inhaling your food because you're running late or engaged in a conversation, looking at your phone, or simply zoning out before realizing you finished your meal? Don't be too hard on yourself. We are a society that is overworked, overstressed, and overburdened. We have to make a conscious effort to separate ourselves from the frantic pace and expectations of our daily lives. In most companies where I've worked, I was expected to take on more responsibilities with fewer resources every year. I could have easily toiled fifteen hours a day and still never finished; I often did just that. There comes a time when you have to know the difference between doing it all and *having* it all. You might be checking items off your list, but are you missing some items that aren't on your list? Like spending time with loved ones? Having moments to just relax with nothing to do but rest or daydream?

When you overextend yourself and multitask on a daily basis, eventually, something has to give. Often it's your nutrition and your health. You skip breakfast or lunch. You eat snacks or dinner from a vending machine. You devour whatever food delivery is brought into a lunch meeting. You go home and barrel through a bag of chips or a pint of ice cream while watching TV, only to be surprised that you've finished the entire container without really remembering eating it. Or if you're like me, and I've done this too many times, you munch on something *while* you're figuring out what to eat for dinner. We've all participated in the mindless, rushed consumption of the wrong food in the wrong environment in the wrong state of mind—or no state of mind at all. When we eat unconsciously, we miss a great opportunity to connect with ourselves, our earth, and the people around us.

Develop a Farmers' Market Mentality

Have you ever seen anyone rush through a farmers' market, grab a fistful of free samples, devour them, then jump in their car and speed out of the parking lot? Of course not. But that's how we eat more often than not. We routinely rush through drive-through windows, eating while driving or at our desks, or sometimes not eating at all. We've become separated from the source and joy of our food by eating food prepared by big corporations. And let's just say that big corporations are a little heavy-handed on the salt, fat, and sugar. Most of us have the antithesis of the farmers' market lifestyle, but it's within our reach.

Imagine strolling casually through a farmers' market and coming upon a sample tray of freshly sliced, ripe peaches. These peaches were once, not too long ago, part of the earth. They are now beautifully presented before you, possibly by the very farmer who grew them. You take one of the toothpicks placed in a small container near the fruit and skewer a voluptuous chunk of juicy, fuzzy peach. You hold it up to your eyes and inspect it, admiring its rich pink-orange flesh. You smell its intoxicating aroma before it reaches your lips. You pop it in your mouth and savor it for a moment, closing your eyes to concentrate on what you are experiencing. You crush the sweet velvety slice with your tongue, teeth, and palate, savoring every moment until the final satisfying swallow. You lick your lips to avoid missing a drop of sweet nectar. You have an appreciation for this little miraculous offering of nature and recognize it as something special. You might even speak with the farmer who carefully arranged the entirety of this bounty before you. As you look around the market, you see the many other farmers and laborers who have worked hard to bring fresh, healthy fare to you, displayed with care and pride, and for a reasonable price. You see people who are living lives of service by nourishing the world and working laboriously each day to give you a gift of good health.

Imagine if you ate every meal, every day, in the same way. Does it sound silly? Unrealistic? We are surrounded by miracles daily and food is one of the greatest miracles of all. The thought that we are eating something that started as a seed, that grew and erupted through the earth as a colorful, delicious, edible package is a miracle, is it not? Simply taking the time to eat mindfully can bring tremendous joy to your life. Taking the time to bring healthy food into your home, your most sacred place, is a blessed event. Respecting your body enough to nourish it is healing. The soothing, purposeful, and methodical act of chopping fresh fruits, vegetables, and herbs while practicing gratitude can be meditative and transcendent. Preparing foods while acknowledging the ritual of cooking can be soothing, methodical, and meaningful if you simply focus on each act of preparation: chopping, slicing, stirring, smelling, tasting, seeing your beautiful finished result (and laughing if it doesn't always turn out so beautifully). Sharing food with your loved ones creates a deep and lasting bond. Enjoying it in solitude is a mindful act of self-love. It is a profound connection to ourselves, our friends, and family, and our earth.

After age forty, it is much easier to understand and appreciate these concepts. We've lived enough of our lives to know that we don't need to be in a cathedral to pray. The cathedral is within us. So, if you've hit the forty-year mark, there are many compelling reasons to make a change. It's easier than you think. You don't have to do it all at once, and you don't have to do it alone. This book is about taking the time you need to make better choices. Be patient and kind with yourself as you would with any new undertaking. There's no rush because this is a lifelong commitment. Each day is an opportunity to recommit to a better way of life.

Not Elimination—*Sublimation*

If you think of veganism as "giving up" what you love, it's definitely going to seem like an impossible goal. Think of it not as giving up your favorite foods, but as substituting your favorite foods with healthier and even tastier plant-based variations. You are adding more delicious, colorful, and nutrient-dense foods, the ability to eat larger amounts of food because fruits and vegetables have just traces amounts of fat and no cholesterol, the ability to eat without counting calories, and increased longevity. Think of it from a point of abundance, not scarcity, and you'll start to understand the beauty of this way of life.

You may have already started cutting back a bit on red meat. You've likely heard about the link between processed meats and cancer. You may be more concerned about cholesterol or illnesses that start to appear with greater frequency as we age like heart disease or Type 2 diabetes. You may want to prepare healthier dinners for your family and don't know where to begin.

We're Here to Help You Every Step of the Way

Susan and I promise you, you won't feel deprived. We're Italian—do you think we walk around starving or eating rabbit food? We promise you'll enjoy the taste of these foods, the textures, and the feeling of satisfaction. I have served these meals to vegetarians, vegans, carnivores, and omnivores and they've all loved the flavor and been amazed at what I've been able to do without meat and dairy. The fact that these foods are healthy ends up being an added bonus for them, too.

Whatever inspires you to try veganism—health, prevention of animal cruelty, environmentalism, a desire to lose weight, or a combination, this book will put you on a path that makes it easy and fun. It seems odd to discuss making eating easy, but when you think about all of the contradictory diets and health directives out there, it's no wonder our nation has become so confused In 2012, a survey of Americans revealed that 52 percent of those polled thought it was easier to do their taxes than to figure out how to eat healthy.[11]

Kindness Begins with Yourself

A vegan life is a life of kindness to animals and the planet. But don't forget to extend that kindness to yourself. We all develop habits over the years that don't go away easily. Our food choices are tied into traditions, like having turkey on Thanksgiving, or eating cake at birthday parties. We won't leave you hanging. This book is filled with foods worthy of holidays, birthday parties, picnics, and other social events, so you won't have to be the odd man or woman out on holidays by having "nothing to eat." What will be more likely is that people will find the food you bring to these events much more interesting and appealing because of the visual appeal and fresh taste of colorful fruits and vegetables. This will make it easier for you to make good choices.

Being kind to yourself means not only putting healthy foods in your body, but forgiving yourself when you fail to do so. If you succumb to temptation and eat a donut or greasy fries, don't start blaming

---

[11] https://www.dosomething.org/us/facts/11-facts-about-american-eating-habits

19

and shaming yourself. Simply say to yourself, *these choices aren't working for me and they're not making me feel good about myself. Next time, I'll choose fresh fruit or vegetables when I feel like I need something satisfying. I deserve to be fit and happy.* By showing respect for your body in your actions and words, you can begin to modify old behavioral patterns and be the recipient of your own kindness.

CHAPTER 3

Getting Started

"Another 2013 study of 44,000 people reported that vegetarians were thirty-two percent less likely to develop ischemic heart disease."
—*Time Magazine*

The reason I believe everyone is a VIP (Vegan in Progress) is because at some point in your day, whether you intend to our not, you're eating something vegan. It's not because you're trying to be vegan; it's because there are so many great tasting foods that happen to be vegan. Have you ever eaten more than a few corn tortilla chips with salsa and guacamole while waiting to order at a Mexican restaurant, or grabbed an apple when walking out the door to go to work? Ever munched on popcorn while watching TV, or taken a bite of your kid's peanut butter and jelly sandwich? Let's face it—there are some delicious plant-based foods out there that you are already enjoying—I call that a starting point!

If you begin by taking a mental inventory of what you're eating each day and acknowledging that you are already enjoying vegan food some of the time, you'll start to see that these foods never feel like a sacrifice. Give yourself credit every time you find yourself eating something vegan. Pay attention and give attention to the good things you are doing. Be a mindful eater. When you catch yourself eating something delicious, healthy, and plant-based, give yourself some well-deserved credit and acknowledgement. Promise yourself to add more fruits and veggies into your diet, and feel good about that promise, because it's one you can easily keep if you keep reading the pages ahead.

Learn the Simplicity and Joy of Substitution

When you read the 52 Ways to Get It Right (page 54), you will learn to omit one non-vegan food item a week, every week of the year. You can slowly approach this lifestyle or jump in all at once—we'll show you how. Just promise yourself you'll try. If you do, it will open a new world of healthy, plentiful eating. Trust me, you won't be hungry because you will have so many options to choose from.

I never feel deprived. I eat a lot of food every day and I don't count calories. In fact, I probably eat more food than the average person because whole, plant-based foods are lower in calories than cheese and meats. Imagine eating more and weighing less without having to count calories. This way of eating brings simplicity to your life. I don't count calories because I eat nutrient-dense food whenever I'm hungry. When I'm not hungry, I stop eating. And it's easier to stop when you're not eating highly addictive processed foods. While there will be some pre-packed vegan foods recommended in this book, they are primarily suggested to help you in your transition. They are helpful when you need to save time or are having a craving for something that is "meaty." Remember, we are working on changing the habits of a lifetime, so we want to be practical in making those changes. We also want to allow the time for the changes you make to become so second-nature that you'll be more likely to stick with them. Cold-turkey diets and other severe diet practices are never sustainable. So don't beat yourself up if you've failed at past diets. Most diets are not structured for success; they're structured for book sales.

Whether you are a vegan, vegetarian, carnivore, or an omnivore, remember that plant-based eating is a celebration. It's a beautiful, kind way of life and one of the easiest ways to be kind to yourself and those around you. We hope you enjoy the recipes contained in this book—they were made with love for you, your family, the animals of this earth, and the planet.

Grocery Shopping

Every effort has been made to offer a list of ingredients that are easily accessible and familiar to non-vegans. Our thought process was to only use foods you could find on a typical Midwestern table like fruits, vegetables, corn, and rice. These foods aren't intimidating. They're familiar and comfortable to most people. There are a few exceptions to the Midwestern table rule, including some packaged vegan foods to help you transition in the most delicious way possible, and other ingredients that are just so good you'll want to have them around through the transition and beyond.

In some cases, we will recommend brand name products that we believe are of superior quality to help you make the recipe taste as it was intended. We did not receive any financial compensation by any companies for doing this; we simply want you to have a good experience when creating these recipes for the first time. Feel free to use ingredients that you feel are comparable such as a favorite canned tomato sauce or a preferred pizza crust.

If you cannot find ingredients at your local grocery store, most any ingredient can be found on Amazon.com. If you really want to be a do-gooder, order from www. smile.amazon.com and a percentage of everything you purchase will go to a charity of your choice; you see, you're already making life-changing choices! Below are some ingredients that may be new to you, but will help you create recipes that are delicious and healthy while still giving you the taste and textures you enjoy. Always consult with your doctor or dietician when starting a new eating plan.

Some New Items for Your Shopping List

Most of the ingredients in this book will be familiar to you. Fruits, nuts, breads, pastas, and grains. Those listed below might be new to you but you will find them to be great staples to have in your kitchen. Always buy the best quality products that make sense for your budget. Organic and non-GMO products are ideal whenever possible. Most companies are starting to label products as non-GMO. Become a label reader and learn which products make the most sense for you.

Raw Agave Nectar: Some vegans eat honey because their veganism is rooted in the nutritious value of raw foods, but for those people who are vegan because of animal advocacy, agave nectar is used instead. You might wonder *what's the harm in eating honey*? The short answer is if we're going to eliminate animals from the food equation, we may as well do it across the board to be consistent. The longer answer is the average bee takes his entire life to produce less than a twelfth of a teaspoon of honey, so we're really putting the little guys to work. Bees need nutrients from their own honey to survive, so when farmers remove honey from their hives and replace it with a sugary substitute, it not only hurts their health, but also messes with Mother Nature (which rarely turns out well). The bees then exhaust themselves as they work overtime to replace the missing honey. Again, you might say *so what? They're just bees*. But, we need bees for our survival, and due to our mass production of honey, the native bumblebee population is declining significantly. Without bees to pollinate crops, we would lose some of the plants we enjoy and prices would surge on other crops as scarcity increases. For example, the California Almond Board claims that without bees, almonds simply wouldn't exist.[12] So, if you could use agave nectar, which is very similar to honey but made from the leaf of a plant, why wouldn't you? It is less viscous than honey; it's also sweeter than honey so you don't need as much. Pure maple syrup (*not* pancake syrup) is another excellent sweetener if you do not have agave. If you have problems with insulin resistance, consult your physician about sweeteners.

Aquafaba: The liquid you usually discard from your cans of beans just got fancy. Aquafaba is the latest trend in vegan eating and once you use it, you won't be tossing the liquid out with the bean can anymore. It's an excellent, cholesterol-free substitute for eggs. Consisting of starches and proteins, it is very similar to egg whites in its texture and binding properties. There are many things that can be made with aquafaba, including meringues and frostings. In this book, we will be using it as an egg substitute in baked goods and

our baked zucchini fry recipe (page 132) that makes French fries seem completely inadequate. For more information on aquafaba, go to www.aquafaba.com.

Cacao: This is one of my favorite ingredients. Not to be confused with cocoa, cacao (pronounced "kuh-COW") is the single richest food source of magnesium on the planet. Raw cacao is created by cold-pressing unroasted cocoa beans to remove the fat and keep the natural plant enzymes alive. Cocoa, cacao's evil twin, is made when the cacao is roasted at high temperatures, destroying much of its nutritional value. When you hear people talk about the benefits of chocolate, they're really referring to the benefits of cacao because this is the healthy, unprocessed part of the plant. Candy bar companies love to cite these studies to increase sales, especially around Valentine's Day. But the fact is, by the time the original plant is processed into a commercial chocolate candy mixed with fatty dairy products and processed sugar, anything of nutritional value is heated out of it. By using cacao, you can have a wonderful rich chocolate flavor and get the nutrients. In addition to being rich in magnesium, cacao has many other health benefits. Studies have shown that it lowers insulin resistance, is high

---

[12]Palmer, Brian, "Would a World Without Bees Be a World Without Us?" NRDC, May 18, 2015, https://www.nrdc.org/onearth/would-world-without-bees-be-world-without-us

in resveratrol, the same antioxidant found in red wine, protects nerve cells, improves heart health, lowers blood pressure, boosts your mood, and contains iron, calcium, potassium, and zinc. So you don't have to give up rich chocolate flavor to be vegan, you just need to upgrade to cacao to get flavor plus nutrients. I like using cacao nibs in my smoothies because it gives texture, but you can also use cacao powder.

Flax Meal: Flax meal is ground flaxseed that provides a good source of fiber and heart-healthy omega-3 fatty acids. It's important to use the seeds in their ground form to maintain maximum health benefits and absorption. You can either buy the seeds and grind them in a coffee grinder or purchase them already ground. In either case, keep them in an air-tight container in the fridge. In this book, we will use flax meal as an egg substitute or "flax egg" by combining 1 tablespoon of flax meal with 3 tablespoons of water and letting it sit in the fridge for twenty minutes. You can use this as a substitute when baking. Several recipes in this book use either flax eggs or aquafaba as egg substitutes. They're both healthy, plant-based alternatives to traditional eggs.

Nutritional Yeast: (a.k.a "nooch") You're not officially a vegan until you have a container of nooch in your cupboard. It's not the yeast that you use to make bread rise, but a deactivated form of yeast that doesn't taste yeasty at all. You'll discover these yellow flakes taste a little like Parmesan cheese when you make some of the vegan cheeses and sauces in this book. It's a great help to people who are transitioning because cheese is hard to give up. You'll be amazed at what you're going to make with this. You'll impress your friends with your Manicotti with Cashew Ricotta (page 206) and other dishes that use this fascinating product. The brand we recommend is Bragg's, which can be purchased online or in health food or specialty food stores.

Nuts: All nuts and seeds used for the recipes in this book should be raw. This is especially important when using them to make cheeses and sauces. Roasting nuts and seeds makes the oil within them rancid. Start to appreciate the taste of fresh nuts. Because nuts and seeds are fats, use them judiciously.

Oils and Fats: Some oils and fats are better than others, but they are still oils and fats. Many people slather food with olive oil because it's a "good" fat, but even good fats should be used sparingly and, according to some experts, should not be used at all. Dr. Caldwell Esselstyn, MD, author of *Prevent and Reverse Heart Disease,* specifically restricts oil completely from his diet plan. If you have heart disease, consult your doctor before using oil as part of your dietary plan. Other doctors suggest that fat should represent 10 percent of your total caloric intake, which is still a very small amount. It is better to get these fat sources through whole plant foods like nuts and avocado rather than processed oils. Because this cookbook is about transitioning, the idea is to work toward the ten percent goal. Note where your fat levels are now, and as you start to make changes towards veganism, the fat levels will drop. When you become vegan, you should continue to drop the percentage of fat until you reach your ten percent goal. We've made an effort to cut back significantly on the oil and fat used in our remake of traditional recipes. The recipes for vegan ice cream are high in fat, using full-fat coconut milk; these are meant to be enjoyed on occasion, in reasonable portions, and not as part of your daily diet. At the end of the book, we will discuss how you can continue to drop the fat content in your diet. We're taking it a step at a time.

In any case, if you are using a recipe that contains oil for breakfast, try a low or no fat lunch. The oils we use most frequently are coconut, olive oil, and small amounts of chili oil to give foods an Asian flair. We also use nuts to make vegan mayonnaise and creamy dressings. These are healthier fats because they contain no cholesterol, but they should still be used judiciously. When you give up meat and dairy altogether, you are eliminating a significant amount of fat and cholesterol from your diet, so eating nuts and avocados is more feasible, but you should still pay attention to your fat intake. Whenever possible, satisfy your sweet tooth with fruit.

Organic Sugar: Regular sugar does not contain animal products but many brands are processed with animal bone char which is kind of creepy even if you're not vegan. There are many great brands. Sugar in the Raw is excellent, but you can use anything labeled organic.

Pasta: While many people consider pasta the enemy, we don't. At my lowest weight I was eating pasta every day, I just didn't douse it in cream sauce. Try a good marinara sauce or the cheese-free pesto sauce in this book. If you have a gluten intolerance, simply substitute gluten free pasta for any of the recipes in this book. You can also choose gluten-free breads for the same reason. Pasta that comes in a box on the shelf is usually vegan, with the exception of egg noodles. Pasta in the dairy section usually contains eggs. Always read the label on the pasta box before you purchase. You'll find that most brands are made with semolina, water, and salt.

Tart Cherry Juice: If you have trouble sleeping at night, take a shot of tart cherry juice. I initially started taking some for its high level of antioxidants, but noticed I would fall asleep within an hour of having just a few tablespoons of it. Tart cherry juice has been associated with many health benefits including fighting inflammation and arthritic pain. It is also a sleep aid; studies have shown that people using tart cherry juice napped less, slept longer, and spent more of their time in bed asleep.[13]

Vegan "Cheeses & Meats": There are a variety of prepacked vegan cheeses and meats that we use in this book because they are great ingredients to help you transition. Companies like Beyond Meat, Gardein, and Field Roast have created excellent low fat, high-protein products that will make you think you're eating meat and dairy. You might be suspicious and wonder if these could ever taste like the real thing. Thankfully, technology has been able to capture the taste and texture of real meats, and these products are ideal for recipes that have that "comfort food" appeal. You'll be surprised at the taste and authenticity of these products. They are also becoming more readily available in grocery stores and large retail stores like Target and online.

Equipment

There are some items that are simply hard to live without once you get used to them. **Blender:** Purchase a good blender within your price range. I'm spoiled and have used high quality blenders like Vitamix and Blendtec for years. These are as good as blenders get. I cannot speak highly enough of Vitamix's quality and their willingness to stand behind their products. I beat my blender into the ground for about five years to the point where it was starting to smell like the motor was burning when I used it. I called them and they told me to send the blender to them. They installed a new motor at no charge and shipped it back to me immediately. Vitamix has the "Accelerator Tampor Tool" that is like a little plunger that helps you push the

[13]http://valleysleepcenter.com/the-truth-about-tart-cherry-juice-and-sleep/

food down while it's blending without the tool touching the blade. Blendtec has a wonderful "twister jar," a top that allows you to scrape the sides of the jar while blending so you can incorporate everything easily. These blenders are not required to make the recipes in the book, but are a joy to use. They're pricey (about $500 and up) so you have to consider what makes sense for you. Handheld immersion blenders are also great for blending soup while it is still in the pot.

Food Processor: Any brand is fine. Susan and I love our Cuisinart. My first one lasted nearly thirty years. It would have lasted longer, but I broke the plastic bowl attachment and couldn't find a replacement part for it because it was so old, but the motor was still working.

Ice Cream Maker: We use a Cuisinart for our desserts but there are many quality brands available.

Spiralizer: This is used to make "pasta" from zucchini and other vegetables. These are about forty dollars and can be purchased online or at most retail outlets that sell kitchen supplies.

Mandoline: This is used to make perfectly even slices and very thin slices. I cannot caution you enough on being safe with this instrument. I cut myself on one of these and it was not fun. It's easy to get into a rhythm while slicing with it and your hand can get in the way. Use the tool that comes with it to grasp the food product; it has a handle that will keep your hands away from danger.

Chef's Knife: If you have good sharp knife you will love cutting fruits and vegetables. I use a Shun—you can get them on sale for about $125 at stores like Williams-Sonoma. Sharpen them regularly; keep them clean and dry. Water and citrus juices will dull your knife's blade faster than anything else. Wipe it after using it and keep it in its protective case.

Nonstick Frying Pan: You can get them at Target or any kitchen supply store. You'll use much less oil, or in some cases no oil, without sticking.

Large, Medium, and Small Pots: You probably own them already.

Baking Dishes: For casseroles.

Sheet Pans, Muffin Pans, and Cupcake Tins: For baking.

Microplane: I use this to zest lemons and grate nutmeg.

Vegetable Peeler: A sharp, new peeler makes all the difference in the world and makes peeling vegetables fun.

Sharp Can Opener: You don't need an expensive one; just a hand operated basic one will do.

Colander: To drain pasta and vegetables

Spatulas and Slotted Spoons

Ice Cream Scoop: Ideal not only for scooping ice cream but for filling cupcake papers and tins with uniform amounts of batter.

CHAPTER 4

✿

Addict Nation

"Cravings are triggered by biological properties of the foods themselves. That is, certain foods have chemical makeups that cause us to crave them in very much the same way that drugs, alcohol, and tobacco have addictive components."

—Neal D. Barnard, MD

"Hello I'm _____ and I'm an addict."
We are a nation of addicts. If you are like many Americans over age forty, it is likely that you are now starting to suffer from the consequences of an addiction. Your addiction is not illegal. It does not leave track marks on your arms. It does not make you stagger into work and pass out at your desk. Your addiction does not impair your driving or cause you to injure or kill innocent people. It does not cause others to judge you and shame you for being an addict. In fact, it's the perfect addiction because no one blames you for it and most people actually encourage it. They even join you in your addiction and celebrate it because they too are addicts. It's the perfect addiction because its signs and symptoms are virtually invisible—at first. As you start to reach forty, however, it gets harder to hide your habit. What was once an enjoyable free-for-all is now a daily vice with dire consequences.

Maybe there was a time when you could quit if you wanted to but now it's hard to quit and you don't want to. The symptoms of your addiction first appear as a little bit of extra bulge around the waistline. No big deal—it's just something that comes with age, right? Then a few extra pounds show up on the scale. But that's to be expected, right? Our metabolic rate drops one percent each year, every year after age thirty.[14]

Refined, processed foods including fast foods stimulate dopamine, the brain's pleasure neurotransmitter. These foods don't just make you feel full, they make you feel high. A high that is similar to that of a drug addict. This high causes binges—cookies, chips, fries, ice cream. Don't believe processed foods are addictive? When was the last time you binged on celery?

Several warning signs along the way revealed themselves but may have been

---

[14]http://www.webmd.com/diet/reverse-middle-age-weight-gain

ignored. When you got your first job, often one that was more sedentary than your life in high school or college, the pounds start to come on. When you got married you gained a little more. No big deal, right? Your friends are getting heavier, too. It's just part of growing up, you tell yourself. Then your doctor happens to mention that your cholesterol is high, but not to worry. There's a pill for that. So you take it, not thinking about what other parts of your health might affected by that pill. After all, your doctor wouldn't give you anything that would compromise your health, right?

After forty, it's harder to lose the weight. When you were young, you could probably skip a meal and drop a pound or two fairly easily. Now, it takes serious effort to lose just five pounds—assuming that's all you have to lose. You look around you and notice that most of your friends are in the same position or worse off and on more medication than you. So it seems normal. And so it should. If everyone around you is an addict and you are enabled to continue your addiction, there's no reason or incentive to change.

If additional ailments arise from your food addiction, there are pharmaceuticals that can take care of it. Heart disease? No problem, there's a pill for that. Diabetes?

High blood pressure? You've got lots of pharmaceutical options. Some of these pills may cause unwanted side effects; constipation, weight gain, and fatigue, to name a few. *But that's okay*, you tell yourself. There are pills for those afflictions, as well. It can be somewhat distressing to be on medication that sometimes makes you feel not quite like yourself. But you can always feel better by engaging in your addiction. A steak dinner. A frosted cupcake from your favorite bakery. A slice of pie for dessert. Salty or sweet snacks. Amped up energy drinks. And anything that includes chocolate. Or bacon. In fact, you can even buy chocolate-covered bacon. Aren't we fortunate to live in a country where anything you desire is a drive-through window or an Amazon-click away?

It seems you know more people who are overweight than you did when you were younger. In some ways, they're the lucky ones. They can see a visible manifestation of their addiction and feel the nagging feeling that they need to do something about it. Maybe they've been told by family or friends that they need to lose weight. Maybe they've been shamed by rude comments from passersby. Shame and embarrassment can be motivators for change, but it's a difficult path to take. The less fortunate in some cases are what I call the sick and thin (SAT). I used to belong to this category. If you are SAT, you feel no shame and no embarrassment because you look healthy. You have no visible signs of your illness. It might take more for you to do something about your diet. It might take a doctor prescribing a pill that you never thought you'd need. Or a diagnosis of colitis, high blood pressure, stroke, or heart attack when you least expected it. Because frankly, you never expected it. You never thought it could happen to you because you've always considered yourself fairly healthy, or at least looked healthy, because the yardstick by which you measure your health is the people around you. And that's a mistake. Remember, everyone around you is an addict. Their addiction to meat, dairy, and processed foods is slowly killing them too—they just don't know it yet. Because the world can't wait to enable each and every one of us to continue our addiction and the denial that accompanies it. Much of the world's livelihood depends on it. So does our entire economy. If we eliminated foods that caused health problems, many food corporations would quickly decline if not collapse, followed by a sharp decline in healthcare industry profits. Our current economy is dependent upon unhealthy,

addicted people. It's a tried and true business model that yields big profits. And you wonder why you have a hard time losing weight, eating right, and getting healthy? Corporate America is working against you every day. They'll taunt you via television ads, internet ads, and strategically placed news articles to use their products. You've been fighting with a corporate giant since you were a child. And giants almost always win. But the David and Goliath story is about to replay itself for those who wish to equip themselves with knowledge and a little faith.

The fight to be healthy and avoid addiction to animal products and processed foods in this day and age is a fight that many are losing, but it doesn't have to be that way. We are living longer, but are we living better? Medical technology is helping us to live with disease instead of preventing it—why would pharmaceutical companies eliminate the very thing that keeps them in business?

But Meat & Dairy Aren't Addictive, Are They?

When you think of addictive foods, you might think of foods with added sugar or fat, like cookies or ice cream. They're definitely addictive but what you may not realize is that meat and dairy are among the most addictive foods on the planet.

Meat and dairy contain elements that bind to and activate the opioid receptors in our brain. This activity results in feelings of euphoria, happiness, and sleepiness as well as a reduction in the sensation of pain. Dairy products have been studied extensively for opioid activity. The protein, casein, in dairy interacts with opioid receptors, creating an addictive response for more. According to Dr. Joel Kahn, founder of the Kahn Center for Cardiac Longevity, "The same medicines used to reverse drug overdoses in emergency rooms can be used to block the desire for cheese."[15] Kahn also cites chemicals in meat that interact with opioid receptors including albumin, hemoglobin, and gamma globulin, stating that when meat eaters were treated with a drug used to block opiate receptors, ham consumption fell by 10 percent, salami by 25 percent, and tuna by 50 percent."[16]

Processed sugar, rice, and gluten also have addictive properties which is why it's important to reduce the consumption of processed foods and adopt a whole food, plant-based diet. Until then, your addiction will rage on. And don't expect any help from the food industry.

Big food companies are fighting against you with compelling advertisements where everything is accompanied by bacon, fat, sugar, or other chemical-laden products. And they're winning. One in four Americans eat some type of fast food every day and 20 percent of meals are eaten in the car.[17] Conveniently packaged and attractively branded foods are all too easy and seductive to pick up. Happy cows promote cheese. Colorful characters dish out clever banter to sell more burgers and shakes. Drive-through windows at fast-food restaurants give us easy access to all the wrong foods and although they now offer "apple slices" with your burger, do you ever get that side order of fruit at the drive-through?

But we can't blame everything on our "I want it now and I want it all" society. Our personal history also plays a role. Our traditions are wrapped up in high-fat, high cholesterol-packages dipped in gravy. Thanksgiving turkey, Fourth of July burgers and hot dogs, Valentine's Day chocolates, Christmas hams, birthday cakes, and Halloween candies punctuate the year with resolutions to eat healthier "after

[15]Kahn, Joel, *Six Foods That Behave Like Addictive Drugs in Your Body,* http://www.mindbodygreen.com/0-14423/6-foods-that-behave-like-addictive-drugs-in-your-body.html
[16]Kahn, Joel, Ibid

[17]https://www.dosomething.org/us/facts/11-facts-about-american-eating-habits

the holiday." But on non-holidays, social and recreational events also provide more opportunities to eat poorly; a baseball game with dogs and beers, a movie with buttery popcorn, or any night dining out because you didn't have time or energy to cook at home. If you feel like you're fighting a losing battle, it's no wonder. You're in a fight, alright. You're backed into a corner and no one's in a rush to get you out of it. It's simply not in their best interest to give up profits, future business, or their own bad habits to help you improve yours.

You may have tried fad diets but they don't last because most diets are not rooted in something sustainable. They all work—if you can commit to them. But few people can because they are addicts. There is a saying among the drug/alcohol addicted community that one is too much and one hundred is not enough. In other words, when it comes to drugs and alcohol, you have to completely avoid them to maintain sobriety because one drink or drug could put you back on the path to destruction and one hundred will never satisfy you because an addict can't get enough.

But what happens when food is your addiction and you have to face it at every turn, not just three meals a day, but every TV commercial, event, movie theater,

website pop-up, concert, billboard . . . and the list goes on. If you've been caught in the junk food vs "I'm trying to eat healthy" cycle, you're not alone. The question is, do you want to change? If you do, I'm here to help. Because I've been there.

I used to be one of the so-called "lucky" ones. I was the person that could eat everything and never gain weight. When I entered college at the age of eighteen, I was 5'10" tall and 125 pounds. My lunch mates in the school cafeteria were a bit envious that I could eat so much and not gain an ounce. Heaps of meatloaf with mashed potatoes and gravy. Cookies, cakes, pies. Two liters of soda a day. I was thin, had long, healthy hair, and a perfect complexion. I didn't exercise—at all. I was a bottomless pit of hunger and I didn't hesitate to feed it. Fast food, junk food, any food. I ate candy every day but didn't have a single cavity.

When I wasn't in school I worked at, of all places, a grocery store, from ages sixteen to twenty-two. What a perfect employment opportunity for a hungry girl. Every day on my break I ate the same thing, a can of soda and two candy bars—every day for six years! And at the end of those six years, I still weighed only 125 pounds.

I could have had the freshest fruits and vegetables available but I wasn't interested. After all, I had no reason to eat healthy food. I was healthy, or so I thought. I continued to eat whatever I wanted with no consequences for my behavior. I finally graduated from college and completed a six-month internship in Northern California. I returned home to Pennsylvania and at the age of twenty-two, for the first time in my life, started to feel a little uncomfortable. I had some rumbling in my stomach—it felt like the flu, but just to be safe, I went to the doctor. I was diagnosed with ulcerative colitis, something I had considered an old man's disease, at age twenty-two. At the time, they could not say definitively if my diet caused the problem—it certainly couldn't have helped. My family had no history of colitis—I was the first.

Whether it was the stress of college, my horrible diet, or a combination of the two, something was clearly wrong and I was put on four different medications immediately. One of the medications was so strong that I slept for eighteen hours a day for three consecutive days before I even realized that the drugs were knocking me out. I had never been on medication before so I had no concept of side effects. The medication regiment coincided with my first job and I actually had to call in sick the second week of work because the drugs made it impossible for me to stay awake. I finally stopped taking one of the four prescriptions and resumed my normal work schedule.

My colitis raged on for decades and would go in and out of remission. Each reoccurrence would vary, ranging from an inconvenient nuisance to a downright debilitating episode. At the age of twenty-five I became a vegetarian, but I didn't do it for health reasons. I did it because I no longer wanted to consume animals. I had always been an animal lover, and after my friend Bobbie introduced me to the concept a few years earlier, I finally made the decision to do it.

I didn't do a lot of homework on being a vegetarian. I just started substituting meat with cheese—bad idea. It made me feel better to know I wasn't causing animals to be killed. Little did I know that the dairy industry was just as cruel if not worse than the meat industry. I was pretty diligent about being a vegetarian. There were a few times when I ate animal products, visiting my grandmother's house and trying her ravioli, or running late for a meeting and grabbing a bacon, egg, and cheese sandwich for breakfast, but ultimately I didn't miss meat any longer and never wanted to go back.

I also did little or no exercise. I gained a little weight but I was underweight to begin with so I didn't worry about it. At 135 pounds I was still thin and looked healthy as ever. I never started exercising until age forty-seven when I started running. My boyfriend at the time, Tom, was a triathlete and he convinced me to run in a 5K race. I huffed and puffed my way through the 3.1-mile course and wanted to continue to run so we could have a shared interest. It also brought out the competitor in me and I thought it would be wonderful to someday run the New York Marathon. I continued running in 5Ks and then a half marathon. When it was time to train for a marathon, Tom and I did a workout program called P90X that combined a strenuous workout program and diet regimen to get in peak physical condition. I followed the vegetarian diet provided with the P90X book and it was quite satisfying. But in month three I noticed that the diet in the program went from vegetarian to vegan. I thought, this might be a good time to try being vegan. I only had thirty days left in the program. And it was quite effortless. I had pasta and spinach for dinner every night. A salad for lunch. Beans for protein. Toast or oatmeal for breakfast. It was a delicious diet and easy to stick with. I had lost significant weight in the third month.

My highest weight as a vegetarian was 150 pounds. With running and the vegan diet combined, I was down to about 128, close to my college weight; too low for my 5'10" frame, but about right for someone who is training for a marathon. I also noticed that I no longer had colitis symptoms. I thought I was just in a long remission, but today at fifty-seven, there are still no signs of colitis. And I've long given up the four medications prescribed to me in my twenty-second year. In fact, I currently don't take any medication at all. Not many people in their late fifties can say that. I credit the vegan diet for helping me, as well as the exercise, although I no longer run anywhere near marathon distances. Today I run two to four miles daily at a leisurely pace and that's just fine with me.

At this point in your life, you have likely determined, as I did; the only diet that works is the one you stick with. I know that plants are the answer to sustainable weight loss, but before you feel defeated and say "I can never do that," keep in mind, I'm the person who spent the first twenty-five years of life eating anything and everything. I do not have will power, never did, never will. I eat amazing food and lots of it. Being vegan allows you to eat a lot of food—good food. It's hard to argue about having both quality and quantity.

This lifestyle is not about starving. It's not about elimination. It's about a whole world of food you may not be aware of. The recipes in this book will give you hope. Many are replicas of the Italian meals my sister and I ate growing up. And trust me, we ate delicious food with an Italian mother, aunt, and two Italian grandmothers doing the cooking. Others recipes are healthy versions of our favorite California cuisine that has so many flavorful culinary influences from around the world.

Eating plant-based foods today is so much easier than it was when I started my journey more than thirty years ago. Today Susan and I are here to make it easy for you to make healthy and delicious choices.

CHAPTER 5

✿

The Plant-Based Un-Diet

"The beef industry has contributed to more American deaths than all the wars of this century, all natural disasters, and all automobile accidents combined. If beef is your idea of 'real food for real people,' you'd better live real close to a real good hospital."
—Neal D. Barnard, M.D., President, Physicians Committee for
Responsible Medicine, Washington, D.C.

Don't consider this a diet book, even though you can easily lose weight on a vegan diet. The main difference between this book and a diet book is that this book focuses on the process, not the outcome. When you are on a diet, you have a goal weight in mind (outcome). So, what's the first thing you do every morning? You get on the scale to see your weight, but you might as well call it a "score." If your weight goes up, you've failed. If it goes down, you've won for that moment and you feel good until the next day when the number may not be what you want it to be, and even if it is, you wonder how long you can persist in this way of life. By using this book, you will focus on the process—making the right choices, eating the right foods for the right reasons, and enjoying what you're eating. You won't be counting calories or keeping score in any way. So you're not going to feel like a failure. After eating in this way, you'll notice your clothes are looser, you don't feel bloated, and you might even find you sleep better at night. Everyone's experience will have its own nuances. Feel free to check the scale, but don't make it a daily ritual that makes you feel bad about yourself.

This book is about making slow incremental changes. In fact, give yourself a year to make the full change. Why? Because if you do it faster than that, you might stumble, which is okay, but you might decide to give up, which is not okay. Look at every day as the "first" day of your diet. What do I mean by that? Bring the same exuberance you've always brought to that first day of every diet you've ever tried.

The Magical First Day

You've been there. The first day of "The _____ Diet". Fill in the blank. Atkins,

Paleo, Low-Carb, No Carb, No Sugar, whichever one you've been on before. Perhaps there were several. Allow me to reenact your experience.

You buy the diet book of the moment. You prepare by cleaning out your cupboards and eliminating the "bad" foods. You go shopping to buy the "good" foods as defined by the book. You make a declaration to your friends and co-workers that you are going on a diet. You might even buy a new lunch container to hold your new magical diet foods. Your first day is approached with diligence and preparation. You go to work armed with your magical foods and special snacks and the resolve that THIS time it's going to work. The book makes it seem so easy. And because you are strong and focused and filled with willpower, the first day of your diet is a success. You ignore the hunger pains and you feel pretty good about yourself. You face the second day with a newfound confidence.

Your second day is strong, but you start to realize that you're embarking on something that's only going to work if you do it every day. And normally, you could resist the temptation, but today is someone's birthday, and there's cake. Would a little bit hurt? It doesn't end at the isolated office celebrations, however.

Can you fend off the vending machine when you've run out of healthy snacks? Your friends are going for pizza later and want you to join them. Should you go and eat a salad while they gorge on thick, cheesy wedges of pie or should you avoid social obligations because there is too much temptation out there?

Why does it have to be so hard to lose the weight and so easy to gain it back? All you can think about is eating. And you know why? Because you're hungry! The first day was easy because you were well-fed the previous day and because you are meant to eat! We all are. You are meant to eat throughout the day and that's okay. You are meant to eat until you feel satisfied. That doesn't mean you lack willpower, it means you are human. Eating throughout the day isn't bad, it's essential. It's just gotten a bad rap because we've stopped eating the food that our bodies need like fruits, vegetables, nuts, seeds, and whole grains and started eating anything and everything that tastes good.

We go on diets because while we're eating junk food we feel strong. Our addiction is being fed, and when you feel strong you make promises. Most junkies vow to get off drugs while they are high because they feel good and confident.

But talk to them when they've gone hours without scoring. They would beg, rob, and steal to get their next hit. And that's why diets don't work. Once you start on the diet, you feel weak and you'll do anything for that next hit of calorie-laden food. You don't have the conviction you had on the first day because you don't have the strength you had on the first day. Because your diet involved deprivation. Because it's asking you to avoid foods that your body craves and needs—carbohydrates and some fats. You didn't fail your diet, your diet failed you.

Eat All Day, Every Day

If you knew your diet didn't restrict the amount of food you ate, every day might feel like the first day—full of hope and ending with success. If you knew you could eat every time you got hungry, it might seem like you had a fighting chance, right? Well, you *can* eat when you're hungry and you *do* have a fighting chance. Because that's the beauty of a plant-based diet. The people I know who eat the most are vegans! They're always eating and talking about eating. Their lives revolve around food because eating is a joy and it is in alignment with their love for animals and the planet. It's a pleasure. There are so many delicious things

to eat and try that they can't get enough. Does that sound like a diet to you?

Another reason they enjoy eating is because most vegans don't count calories; they don't have to. They've eliminated two of the biggest calorie hogs out of their diets, meat and dairy. If you did nothing but eliminate meat and dairy from your diet and added fruit, veggies, grains, and pasta—yes, pasta—you'd probably lose weight immediately, assuming you didn't douse your food in oil or other fats.

Does that sound horrible? Eating bread, is that so bad? I'm not saying you should eat a loaf of bread a day, but how many diets have you been on that made bread and pasta the enemy? I'm here to tell you, they're not. You can and should have quality whole grain breads, pasta, and even potatoes. If you prefer gluten-free bread and pasta, that's fine. Starting to sound doable? It is. Remember, I'm the girl who has zero willpower, and I don't need it. I eat a lot of food every day. And it's a good way to live. In fact, it's the only way to live. We were not meant to be deprived.

How to Never Fail

First you have to change your definition of failure. Remember when I told you earlier that you are an addict? Part of recovery from addiction is a word called "recidivism."

It means that when most addicts try to quit the drug they're on, they relapse. It happens a lot. In fact, relapse rates for addicts range from 50 to 90 percent.[18] If you've ever spoken to someone who gave up smoking, drinking, or drugs, they will likely tell you they didn't quit successfully the first time. But, it's important to note that a relapse doesn't mean failure unless you stop trying. It's part of the process, and if you acknowledge the relapse and get right back on track, you will find that each time you get back on track you will become stronger in your ability to stick with it.

When you think about kicking food addictions, we might not get it right the first time either, and that's okay. What counts is that you keep working at it and make a lifelong commitment to eating the right way. If you make the commitment lifelong, your life can get longer.

Why You Can Succeed with This Diet: The Recycling Analogy

This book is customized to how you like to do things because I believe everyone can be successful with any new challenge as long the they set up a structure for success.

If you currently recycle, you can probably remember a time when you didn't. Were you a bad person for not recycling? No, but chances are in the beginning you had to take your recyclables to some out-of-the-way location that wasn't convenient. Now, you might have a special recycling bin that you put in front of your house and it's picked up along with the garbage. The bins serve as triggers for better behavior and they are visible and convenient, enabling you to keep your promise to recycle. Did you suddenly become a good person, or even a different person now that you're recycling? No, you're the same person, but now it is easier to recycle so you do it and you feel better about your choices.

Being vegan is no different. You're going to be the same person, but this book will make it easy for you to stay healthy and slim down in a convenient way that does not go against the grain of your daily life. The delicious recipes will reinforce your healthy choices so that you'll want to make them regularly. When you make healthy choices, you'll feel better, and when you feel better, you'll make healthier choices.

[18]http://alcoholrehab.com/addiction-recovery/beating-the-relapse-statistics/

Relapse is Not the End—It's an Important Part of the Process

What happens if you relapse and you eat something that's not vegan or unhealthy like greasy fries or a fast food burger with bacon? Remember the recovering drug addict. Most addicts in recovery didn't get it right the first time. That doesn't mean you should plan to fail.

That just means you're going to have moments when you're tempted to eat meat. If you give in to those temptations, don't beat yourself up because that's going to result in a downward spiral. Instead, notice how your body feels when you eat something you're not supposed to eat. You might feel bloated or tired. Just take note of how you feel when you eat healthy foods and unhealthy foods and vow to make better and different choices with each meal.

Another change to be aware of is that if you go vegan for a while, you'll notice you have almost no body odor. When you eat meat, a stronger odor will return and you'll wonder how you never noticed it before. Start noticing how you feel when you eat healthy vegan food, physically and psychologically, and how you feel when you don't. Eventually, your body will reward you for eating the right thing.

The relapse is when most people give up. Instead of giving up, see it as an important part of the process, an opportunity to notice that you feel better when you eat better, and recommit to eating better. In fact, recommit every day to making good choices before you put one thing in your mouth. Also commit to how you will structure your path for success. There are three main pathways on how to approach this way of eating.

Three Pathways to Success Based on Your Personality Type

1. The Fast & The Furious: Are you the first person to jump into a swimming pool without first dipping your toe in the water to check the temperature? If so, this path is for you. In fact, you don't even need to read this book. You just need to do one thing: Eliminate all animal products and oils from your diet. That's it. This one sentence is all you need to lose weight, keep it off, improve your health, and have significantly less of a negative impact on the planet. Most of you won't believe me, but it's been scientifically proven. It's even likely you will be able to reduce your medications as the pounds come off and the cholesterol goes down, but please never do that without your doctor's consent.

You should try this path if you are one of those strong minded people who can put mind over matter and never look back. I'm not one of those people, but if you are, go for it. I would love to hear your success story. Once you complete this book, this is the ultimate state you should strive for. But this book is about *transitioning* to that way of life.

2. The Cautious & Curious: If you're not on the Fast & Furious path, that's okay; you have options. Maybe you're the "look before you leap" type and like doing research on diets before you make a full commitment. I can respect that. For you, incorporating vegan meals into your diet just one day per week will likely be the path that works for you. The thing I like about this path is it that it's like recreating the "first day" of any diet. You will likely be very successful on that one day per week because you'll do everything you did on every other diet and you'll know that tomorrow you can go back to your normal way of eating, as long as it's not gorging on greasy foods, fatty foods; you've got to keep it within reason.

This path can also be referred to as "meatless Monday." The benefit of meatless Monday is that most people think it is not only doable, but enjoyable. It's something novel; it gives them an opportunity to try new foods and they feel good about it.

If you've ever said, "I'm craving Chinese food today," or "I feel like Italian food today" just think of meatless Monday in the same way. "I'm going to eat vegan today." See it as simply a category of dining you're going to enjoy as a break from your normal routine.

If this is the only thing you can do, it's a great start. You can go to the recipes in this book and know that you're doing something good for your health and the planet one day a week. You might even find that you enjoy some of the recipes so much that you want them on more than one day a week. The more meatless days you do, the better for your health, your waistline, and the environment. Meatless Monday is a good way to ease into veganism, but try not to undo the good you've done on Monday by eating more meat and dairy on Tuesday or the rest of the week. In fact, try to extend Meatless Monday a little by simply adding more veggies into your meal for the rest of the week. Keep adding until your meat and dairy portions are less.

For example, if you were going to eat spaghetti with meatballs on Tuesday, have one less meatball and add some sautéed spinach. Or have no meatballs and add a big serving of salad before you eat. Enjoy a luscious berry smoothie for breakfast. Munch on apples or pears or any fruit or veggies between meals. Eat a handful of almonds when you're hungry. Don't deprive yourself. If you're hungry, it's okay to eat. Just make sure it's hunger you're feeling and not anxiety, boredom, depression, or some other feeling. Being mindful of why you are eating is crucial. Ask yourself if you're really hungry or just bored sitting at your desk, and if you are hungry, eat until you're satisfied, not stuffed.

This way of life is not about limitations, it's about adding more delicious, healthy foods. The only restriction is that fats should make up ten percent of your daily caloric intake. Some more conservative experts say 20 to 35 percent of your caloric intake can be from fat. Think about where you are now and plan to move in the direction of the ten percent.

Chances are there are some fruits and veggies you enjoy eating. Stock up on the best fruits and vegetables of the season and always have them available. You will never or feel deprived when you can eat any time you are hungry. These are not huge changes, just little things to keep the magic happening. You'll feel a difference and you will soon start to notice a difference.

3. The Cool & Cantankerous: If you're in this category, nobody's going to tell you how to eat. And you're not going to make any changes on someone else's time schedule. You make your own rules when you want to at a pace that works for you.

Most people I know fall into this category. They are on a slow and steady path to eliminating meat and dairy. And they feel good about it. These are people who say to me, "I don't eat red meat anymore," or "I rarely have dairy anymore and I noticed my stomach feels better." They have slowly started to eliminate the things they feel they can do without. And they realized they don't miss what they've eliminated. In fact, they started to feel better, and some lost weight right away.

I have a friend who simply started by replacing the milk in her coffee with creamers made with almond or coconut milk. This was such a small change, but she started feeling better right away. She noticed that her stomach wasn't bothering her anymore. She also lost about five pounds rather quickly. She enjoyed the taste of the creamer as well. She simply introduced a new product into her life and realized she liked it and didn't miss the old product.

This is the theme behind slow and steady. If this is a style that you can relate to, read the 52 Ways to Get It Right (page 54) to get you started. It is such a gradual change that you can easily transition without feeling like it's an imposition on your current lifestyle.

Seven Steps for Success

All three of the above paths will work and one in particular will work for you depending on your personality type and your way of incorporating change into your life. Regardless of which path you take, there are some key rules:

1. Be patient: You didn't develop a food addiction overnight and you won't change your eating habits overnight.

2. Acknowledge, honor, and celebrate every change you make: Each change is a big deal because it's a stepping stone to a better and healthier life. By simply changing the cream in your coffee to almond or coconut milk, you've not only created a good habit, you've set the groundwork for other good habits. You've proven to yourself that you can make modifications without feeling like you're making a huge sacrifice. Remember the recycling story— once you find out how to make the change convenient, you'll realize you can do this!

One change at a time can make this a very easy, progressive change. I don't want anyone to feel like the rug was pulled out from under them. I want everyone to feel like they've taken a triumphant step on a path toward health.

3. Stumble forward: One of the biggest mistakes people make in starting anything new is that if they fail, they develop an "all or nothing" mentality. Well, I screwed up on my diet so I guess I'll eat that entire chocolate cake now. Stumbling is part of succeeding. If you realized that you are feeling the effects of the addictive properties of junk foods and animal products, you will acknowledge that quitting cold turkey rarely happens. Addictions keep coming back if you indulge them. If you acknowledge them as addictions and move on by being kind and understanding with yourself and being more prepared to handle obstacles the next time, you'll get through it.

4. Practice praise and gratitude: Every time you eat something vegan, think about the flood of healthy nutrients you are putting into your body. It's better than any prescription drug out there. It's whole, nutrient-dense food that is here for the taking. Have gratitude for the beauty of the good food you have access to. Realize that people in some parts of the world will never enjoy some of the healthy options that are so readily available to you. I am in awe of how fortunate we are to have grocery stores filled with beautiful produce, farmers' markets with whole, plant-based foods, and the ability to have products shipped to us if they are not local. We live in an amazing and abundant society. Be grateful every time you choose to eat something healthy. Praise yourself for breaking away from the addiction mentality that permeates our nation. Praise your newfound "sobriety" and the fact that you are making more thoughtful choices. Post your food choices and stories on our Facebook page at www. facebook.com/40YOV to get some extra support and kudos from a community of like-minded people.

5. Become a vegan detective: My friends Rochelle and Melissa will often call me and say, "Did you know this brand of English Muffins is vegan? I bought some for you!" They've inadvertently become vegan detectives just because they always want to have food for me to eat when I visit them. I love them for that. In doing so, they've often tried the products themselves and realized how delicious they are.

They've found creamy vegan ice creams and cheeses, hearty breads and cereals, and so much more. And when they find them, they simply add them to their cupboards and have something new and exciting to reach for when they're hungry. Simple little changes. Being a detective will also surprise you when you find products you didn't think were vegan that ARE vegan. Those are big wins. One of my favorite brands of jarred pasta sauce, Classico Tomato & Basil Sauce, happens to be vegan and it's what I use when I don't have time to make my own homemade sauce. Some amazing breads in the grocery store bakery are vegan as well, but they're not always labeled as such. You'll also find some products you thought were vegan that are NOT. I have found vinaigrette salad dressings that contain milk, marinara sauces that contain cheese, and minestrone soups that contain beef stock. So being a detective can be very informative.

While it's always best to eat whole, plant-based foods, sometimes you're going to want to buy a can of soup or something out of convenience. Always try to choose products that contain ingredients you can pronounce and are not high in fat or overloaded with salt. So become a label-reading vegan detective and enjoy learning about what you're eating.

6. Have fun: Clip vegan recipes from magazines or go online and find countless others. Buy vegan cookbooks. Make it a fun project for yourself and the family to test new products. Think of the example you'll be setting for your children, family members, and friends when you introduce them to something delicious.

6. Begin changing your junk food habits: Let's face it, junk food is tempting for vegans and omnivores alike. I'm not going to encourage you to eat junk food, but if you have to have it, minimize the negative impacts as much as possible. If you are at the movie theater and you forgot to bring a snack, get popcorn without the butter. Popcorn is a whole grain and not a junk food at all, but we've turned it into one by adding butter and way too much salt. If you want to get candy, get the Red Vines or Twizzlers licorice; at least they're vegan and animals didn't have to suffer for that snack.

Better yet, get out of the habit of eating while watching a movie. It's a hard habit to break, I'll admit. I just want you to feel like you have a way out even if it's not ideal. Most of the time we eat in movies out of habit. We're used to munching on something while we watch and it's now become part of the movie experience, but you can break that association by simply not eating while the movie is taking place. In doing so, you'll develop new associations with the movie such as talking with the person you came with, checking in on Facebook that you're watching the movie, or simply watching the trailers for the upcoming show. Remember, we're breaking addictions and have to develop new habits to replace the old ones.

CHAPTER 6

Exercise:
The Plain and Simple Truth

"The secret of getting ahead is getting started."
—Mark Twain

This will probably be the shortest chapter you've ever read about exercise. Because there's not a lot to say other than you've got to do it. You've got to move and you've got to do it every day. Here's the good news. You don't have to be a triathlon champion. You don't have to run a six-minute mile. You just have to move to get your heart pounding a little faster than it does when you're resting and you have to do some load-bearing exercise. This is not just about weight loss. If you stop moving, it's going to be harder for you to maintain your weight. It will be harder for you to get up from your chair, to get in and out of a car, to bring your groceries into the house. If you stop moving, you start dying. It's that simple.

Just like the recycling story, if it's not convenient, you're not going to do it. This applies to exercise. Find a way to make exercise convenient. You don't have to join a gym, unless it's a gym that's in your office and it's easy to get to on your lunch break or after work. You don't have to buy exercise equipment unless you like exercise equipment and you're going to use it. If you prefer exercising alone, do it alone. If you prefer being with people, join a class and bring a friend who will make you go to class even if you don't want to. The point is, do it and find a way to enjoy it. And remember, you don't have to be champion athlete. You just have to be consistent. You don't even have to be consistently perfect. When I run, I'm not running a six-minute mile. I'm a slow runner. But I know if I use that as an excuse and stop running, I'll end up being an even slower runner and then a non-runner and then a couch potato.

I've hated exercise for as long as I can remember. And because I was always tall and thin, I didn't need to do it to lose weight. So I didn't. In fact, I didn't start seriously exercising until I was forty-seven and even then I only did it because my boyfriend was an athlete and I ran in a 5K (3.1 mile) race in order to participate in an activity with him.

No one was more surprised than I was when I fell in love with running. While running the 5K race, I got hooked. Not because of the running itself, at least not at first. It was specifically because of what was happening around me while I ran. To the right of me was a mother walking her blind twelve-year-old daughter through the course. It broke my heart, knowing that this mom was trying to instill confidence in this young girl, who would someday have to face the world without a mom. I can only imagine how much the mother wanted to teach this little girl about the importance of setting goals, achieving milestones, and not letting a disability stand in her way. To the left of me the marine corps was running in unison singing an appropriate cadence, "We are running just for fun, we won't stop until it's done . . . " Leaving me in the dust was a man in his seventies holding a long flagpole bearing the American flag high above his head. All around me I witnessed people running at their own pace for their own reasons and I ultimately fell in love with running because of what it represented. It's a sport for all ages, all motivations, and all abilities.

I finished the 5K and someone put a medal around my neck. My boyfriend greeted me at the finish line (he was done in a fraction of the time that it took me). I was hooked. And proud. I still run to this day. I was by no means the fastest runner then and am still not now—I never will be. I prefer a leisurely pace because what I love about running is the same thing I loved about that first race. It allows me to see the beauty that is happening around me. I get to people-watch, witness the beauty of nature; run alongside the Pacific Ocean where I live or in the beautiful green hills of Pennsylvania when I visit Susan. I went on to run the New York Marathon at the age of fifty and it was an absolute joy. Again, I saw people running for every reason under the sun; raising money for charities, getting in shape, preparing for a high school reunion. The reason didn't matter, what mattered is they had a reason. They had a "why." And so must you.

It's been said that we can endure any "what" if we have a "why." Finding your "why" will make exercising easier because you will see it as a means to something greater and loftier than just going through the motions of something that's supposed to be good for you.

The "why" is the only thing that will make it convenient, enjoyable, and sustainable. Do it to socialize with your friends. Do it because it's the only time of day you can listen to your favorite tunes without being interrupted by phone calls or kids. Do it because it's quiet time that gives you time and space to think. Trust me, I've tried every exercise under the sun and hated all of them: yoga, Pilates, jazzercise, you name it. If I hadn't tried running, I never would have known how much joy it would bring to my life.

I run on the beach in the morning and listen to my favorite music on my iPhone. I will only allow myself to listen to my running music mix *while* I'm running. I can't sit on the couch and listen to it. That in and of itself is a motivator because in order to listen to my favorite upbeat tunes,

I have to run. Find tricks and treats if you have to, but find a reward system that is not related to food.

In addition to listening to my favorite music, I have other "whys" that keep me motivated. I am filled with gratitude that I can see the ocean every day, smell the salty air, see others running or walking on the beach with their dogs and kids. I love smelling the wonderful aroma of restaurants cooking breakfast and enjoying the beauty around me. I don't need special equipment, just my iPhone, earbuds, and a water bottle. I always run alone. It's like meditation for me. I run for two to four miles at a time. No one talks to me. No one interrupts my thoughts. No one asks me for anything. I turn my phone on "do not disturb" because I don't take calls during my run time. I look forward to it and if I'm tired some days and I need to walk part of the way that's okay. Learn to live in the gray areas and your life will be so much easier.

There was a time when I wanted to improve my running time so badly and if I didn't reach a certain distance per minute I would feel like a failure. I ran while looking at my watch and constantly checked my heart rate and speed. What a missed opportunity. Those things are helpful if you're training for a race, but I don't race anymore and I don't care if I'm the fastest runner in my age group. If you enjoy that sort of thing, it's great, but it's not essential. That black and white thinking did not help me feel good about running five, ten, or even twenty-six miles! Enjoy what's happening around you. Make exercise a practice that gives you joy and you'll want to do it more.

Find reasons to take walks during the day if possible. There was a woman who operated a fresh fruit stand a few blocks from the building where I used to work in LA. This was not just any fruit. It was the most amazing fruit ever. All the fruit was cut fresh while I waited. I watched her skillfully and quickly slice fresh chunks of pineapple, mango, and watermelon. It made me motivated to walk to her cart and get something healthy for lunch. It was a reward and it felt good to get outside and walk in LA—a city more known for its freeways than its foot traffic. I still marvel after more than thirty years of living in California that I am able to work in this amazing city with skyscrapers and faces I've never seen, so close to Hollywood and Beverly Hills and every activity and type of person imaginable. It's not only different from where I was raised in Pennsylvania, it's different from where I live in Orange County, about fifty miles away. I still marvel at the beauty of Los Angeles and always will. And that gets me walking and eating some picture-perfect fresh fruit. Both diet and exercise can be made more meaningful, enjoyable, and even spiritual if we create the right mental framework.

See how creative and appreciative you can be as you choose healthy foods and find ways to move and break a sweat. Make choices that resonate with you, fit within your schedule, and are effective as well as reasonable. You've got this!

Don't wait for perfection to get started. Just get started and work to improve. Anything you're good at is something you probably do every day or almost every day. Driving, your job, cooking, playing an instrument. Practice makes permanent— not perfect. Because you might not always be perfect in the way you practice, or exercise in this case. Do it anyway and do your best. Eventually you will be doing it permanently and will become better for it.

PART II

CHAPTER 7

52 Ways to Get It Right: Leaning in to Veganism

"All changes . . . have their melancholy; for what we leave behind us is a part of ourselves; we must die to one life before we can enter another."

—Amy Cuddy, *Presence: Bringing Your Boldest Self to Your Biggest Challenges*

Most popular diets are a shock to your system. If you've been eating all the wrong foods and you suddenly have to start eating all the right foods, even if they're super healthy foods, you struggle because everything you've known, loved, and found comfort in has been taken away from you. You're going through withdrawal. Even if you feel healthier or lighter, your bad habits don't disappear because you suddenly started a diet.

I'm a practical person and a junk food junkie by nature. I know two things. First, you can't change a bad habit unless you replace it with a good habit that's easy, convenient, and has a payoff. And second, you can't change all of your bad habits all at once in a permanent way.

That's why I've created a system that will allow you to change slowly, over time.

In fact, you can take a year on this. This was designed to replace your habits, one at a time, and give you an opportunity to succeed while not feeling deprived. You might think taking a year is too long to lose weight. But if you look at popular diets, people often lose weight the first month, then a year later are back to their same weight or even more. With our system of eating, you will gradually lose weight and keep if off, so a year from now, you are likely to be thinner than the fad diet person who initially dropped a lot of weight, and you will have the skills to keep the weight off by making simple changes, one at a time.

Author and social psychologist Amy Cuddy in her book *Presence*[19] presents a powerful case for something she calls

---

[19] Cuddy, Amy, *"Presence: Bringing Your Boldest Self to Your Biggest Challenges"*, Little Brown & Company, December 2015

"self-nudging," a process of setting small, achievable goals instead of a large goal that may be unrealistic. This is a powerful tool, but one we often don't think to use because in our goal-oriented society, it's more exciting to claim a big, sexy goal, than a small incremental one. But you don't have to proclaim any goals when eating the 40-Year-Old Vegan way. This chapter is about taking steps so incremental that they're pretty unremarkable—not in a bad way, but in a way that you can do it and not feel like you're making a monumental change that you have to announce to the world. And in doing so, these little weekly "nudges" will help you achieve the health and weight loss that may have eluded you until now.

For example, in Week 1, you are asked to use milk substitutes like cashew or almond milk in your cereal or coffee. That's all you have to do in Week 1. So you might have cereal with almond milk, scrambled eggs, and even bacon. Week 1 says nothing about giving up meat because the goal is to make one small change at a time. Having a week will also give you a chance to try different brands to see which one you like the most. Some people prefer creamy cashew milk, others like a lighter almond milk.

In Week 2, you will continue to use the milk substitute, and will be asked to use bread that does not contain any animal products like butter or eggs. Your current brand of bread might already be vegan, but it's important to read your labels. You will do this while still incorporating the milk substitute, which you've now been doing for one week. You've started to get used to substituting milk, so it's going to be easier to do it the second week, while starting with your next substitution. You might use your new bread and still have a slice of turkey on it because I haven't yet asked you to give up turkey. So you're not going to feel a significant deprivation because this is happening slowly and methodically. Each week is cumulative and builds on the week before. By the time you get to the last week of the program, you will have built up your "habit muscle" and will have a fighting chance. You'll also be a vegan—yes, you! And you're not making changes that are painful. One week, you'll be asked to substitute the mayo on your sandwich with avocado or hummus. That's an upgrade as far as I'm concerned! How many diet books allow you to eat avocado and hummus?

If you're an overachieving type and you want to take it two weeks at a time instead of one, go for it. Similarly, if you want to make one change every two weeks, you can do that as well. It will take two years to transition, but you'll still be moving in the right direction. Know that eating habits don't happen in a day, and they won't change in a day, so go at a pace that feels comfortable for you.

Also, acknowledge and celebrate every change you make. It's a big deal to change a habit, and you want to give yourself credit not only for making a positive change in your life that's good for your health, but for knowing that you have practiced a kind act. You have helped and will continue to help save animals and our planet. Truly try to comprehend that your gesture has not gone unnoticed. Your actions make a difference in the world and your cumulative actions make a bigger difference. These are small steps that will not seem like sacrifices because of how you are doing them and the fact that you are taking it slowly. Some weeks will be easy for you and other weeks may take a bit more willpower, but I'll never ask you to omit something without substituting something else—that's only fair! With each passing week, we're simply replacing one habit with another one that is easy, sustainable, and enjoyable.

This plan will help you avoid two of the pitfalls you have encountered with previous diets. First, it will prevent you from having to change all bad eating habits at once because it's a step-by-step program. Second, it will give you a substitute for what you have tried to give up before so you won't feel deprived.

You might notice, as many of my friends have, that when you give up certain foods, you feel less stomach distress. Foods like dairy and cheese or heavy meat products often don't agree with us. Bloating, indigestion, or irregularity are just a few ways our body tries to tell us something. As you work your way through the chart, make notes on any changes you see or feel in your body. Has bloating disappeared? Are you more regular? Are your clothes getting looser? You'll be surprised at how small changes can make such a big difference. It's important to take note of these positive changes because they will reinforce your food choices and make you more likely to stay on track.

All you have to do is take this one step, one week, and one bite at a time. You can do it in the order written or you can skip around. It doesn't matter, as long as it works for you. Check the box at the end of each week when completed and put the date of completion so you can see tangible evidence of your progress. There's something satisfying about completing a checklist. Enjoy the journey!

52 Weeks to Vegan
The Meal Plan

*Please see resources (pg. 272) for a complete listing of product references

Week	Instead of	Try This	Date When Completed	Note any positive changes you feel as a result	Recipe to try this week
Week 1	using milk in your cereal, coffee, or as a beverage	use milk substitutes: almond, coconut, cashew, hemp, or soy. Try several to see which ones you like. Check out Silk and So Delicious brands.			Coconut, Pecan & Apricot Granola (pg. 77) ☐ *Check!*
Week 2	using bread that contains animal products such as milk, cheese, or honey	choose from the many breads that do not contain animal products. You might find that your current bread choice is already vegan, but do the research. Ezekiel Sprouted Grain Bread is a wonderful, dense, and satisfying bread you may want to try. Experiment with different breads until you find your favorite.			Chestnut, Fennel & Avocado Crostini with Orange Essence (pg. 114) ☐ *Check!*
Week 3	eating the usual meals offered on long flights while traveling	request the vegan meal. They are usually infinitely better than the regular fare. Now this is an easy week if you're not traveling, but keep in mind, you need to keep this rule for future trips.			Chocolate Surprise Breakfast Cupcakes (pg. 101) ☐ *Check!*

Week	Instead of	Try This	Date When Completed	Note any positive changes you feel as a result	Recipe to try this week
Week 4	your usual meat-filled burrito	replace the meat with beans. Make sure they're not cooked in lard. Most restaurants are getting better at offering beans that are not cooked in lard. Notice you have not yet been asked to give up cheese. I'm not taking away everything all at once. Just replace the meat with the beans.			Unstuffed Poblano Pepper with Macadamia Cheese (pg. 228) ☐ *Check!*
Week 5	putting mayonnaise on your sandwich	try hummus or mashed avocado. Delicious and decadent. Just a little goes a long way. You can also use a vegan mayo substitute like Hampton Creek Just Mayo, which is dairy-free and Non-GMO.			Grown Up Mac & Cheese Casserole (pg. 214) ☐ *Check!*
Week 6	indulging in milk chocolate	eat a good quality dark chocolate. Read the label to make sure that no dairy has been added. Another option is to add cacao to your smoothies to give them a delicious chocolaty flavor. Check out Ojio Raw Organic Cacao Nibs or Powder. I love putting two tablespoons of cacao nibs in my smoothie for a luscious chocolaty taste.			Funky Monkey Smoothie (pg. 92) ☐ *Check!*

Week	Instead of	Try This	Date When Completed	Note any positive changes you feel as a result	Recipe to try this week
Week 7	a breakfast that contains bacon or sausage	choose oatmeal topped with chopped walnuts, blueberries, a little cashew milk, agave nectar, or maple syrup. It will taste like dessert. Or purchase a vegan bacon or sausage substitute if you really feel the need to have a "meaty" breakfast. You can have this along with your scrambled eggs if you wish because you haven't yet been asked to omit them. See what we did there?			Raspberry Purée (pg. 85) ☐ Check!
Week 8	your usual meat-filled sandwich	make an AB&J sandwich with a good quality almond butter and fruit preserves. When you're not paying the expense of meat products, you can get top quality nut butters and preserves. There's nothing like a good AB&J to make you feel like a kid again.			Mashed Sweet Potato Tacos (pg. 238) ☐ Check!
Week 9	thickening your homemade soup with cream	use puréed, cooked vegetables instead. This can include potatoes, cauliflower, or yams. Toss them into the soup pot and use an immersion blender. You'll have a thick creamy soup without the fat, calories, or cholesterol.			Thai Coconut Soup with Lime & Cilantro (pg. 150) ☐ Check!

Week	Instead of	Try This	Date When Completed	Note any positive changes you feel as a result	Recipe to try this week
Week 10	traditional pancakes or waffles for breakfast	try our vegan pancakes! In chapter 8 you'll find creamy, satisfying smoothie recipes. They're a great way to wake up and give you sustained energy!			Banana Pancakes with Blueberry Basil Purée (pg. 86) ☐ Check!
Week 11	honey in your tea	use agave nectar. It's a natural sweetener that's sweeter than sugar so you don't need much. This is easy! You can do this.			Christmas Muesli (pg. 81) ☐ Check!
Week 12	buttering your bread at a restaurant	just ask for a small dish with balsamic vinegar and dip away; you'll be hooked. No olive oil necessary.			Citrus Quinoa Salad with Toasted Hazelnuts (pg. 182) ☐ Check!
Week 13	grabbing a candy bar for a snack	rediscover the joy of eating a freshly peeled orange. This sounds silly but you have to try it. Peeling the skin from an orange releases a beautiful spray of orange essence; take the time to see and smell it. Peeling an orange slows you down and allows you to have a moment to appreciate this natural food. There's something magical about eating an orange.			Kale Salad with Orange Vinaigrette (pg. 192) ☐ Check!

Week	Instead of	Try This	Date When Completed	Note any positive changes you feel as a result	Recipe to try this week
Week 14	adding ground beef into any recipe	use Beefy Crumbles by Beyond Meat. They are low in fat and will take on the flavor of any spices or sauces you use with them. There are several recipes in this book using Beyond Meat products.			Grandma's Stuffed Pasta Shells (pg. 236) ☐ *Check!*
Week 15	topping your burrito, sandwich, or anything else with cheese	either omit the cheese altogether or try some great cheese substitutes like Field Roast Vegan Chao Cheese Slices, Miyoko's Kitchen, or Kite Hill.			Salad Hoagie Recipe (pg. 123) ☐ *Check!*
Week 16	using whipped cream to top dessert	try So Delicious Brand Coco Whip Topping. It's so creamy and has a subtle coconut flavor that makes a great topping for any dessert.			Banana Coconut Cupcakes (pg. 249) ☐ *Check!*
Week 17	eating an ice cream cone or novelty bar	enjoy amazing frozen treats like So Delicious Dairy Free Coconut Milk Ice Cream. Better yet, freeze some bananas and toss them in a blender with a little water and vanilla to make your own "nice" cream. You'll love our homemade "nice cream" recipes.			Blackberry "Nice" Cream (pg. 253) ☐ *Check!*

61

Week	Instead of	Try This	Date When Completed	Note any positive changes you feel as a result	Recipe to try this week
Week 18	going to a fast food burger restaurant	go to Subway and get a sub on a traditional white roll made with ALL of their vegetables. No meat or cheese. They have such a wide variety of veggies, your bun will runneth over! You can also make one of our great sandwiches or wraps from chapter 9.			Tacos Verdes (pg. 233) ☐ *Check!*
Week 19	sautéing vegetables in butter	use vegetable broth with minced garlic. Sauté until vegetables are tender. Add a little salt and fresh ground cracked pepper. You won't miss the butter at all. I sautéed spinach like this for a non-vegan friend and she was hooked! She had no idea you could get so much flavor into a green leafy vegetable!			Broccoli & Pasta (pg. 205) ☐ *Check!*
Week 20	eating cheese for a snack	try air popped popcorn. It's a whole grain and will fill you up. If you don't have time for a popper there are bagged brands of air popped corn that are low in calories and delicious. You can eat quite a bit because of the low calorie content. Keep some at work, in the car, or anywhere you might be tempted to snack.			Zucchini Fries with Ranch Dressing (pg. 132) ☐ *Check!*

Week	Instead of	Try This	Date When Completed	Note any positive changes you feel as a result	Recipe to try this week
Week **21**	having a BLT or turkey club sandwich	have an ALT sandwich, or avocado, lettuce and tomato. No mayo necessary. The avocado provides the fat. Add a little salt and pepper or hot sauce.			Avocado & Tomato Toast (pg. 95) ☐ *Check!*
Week **22**	munching on M&M's or other candy	snack on edamame (soybeans). You can purchase a bag of frozen soybeans still in the pod and microwave them. Top with sea salt and enjoy. You'll feel so much better when you eat a healthy protein source and won't have the sugar drop you get with candy. These are conveniently packaged so you can bring them to the office.			Asian-Style Dumplings (pg. 212) ☐ *Check!*
Week **23**	going to a friends for dinner, then discovering there's meat on the menu	offer to bring something that you can eat that others will enjoy. You can put it together quickly and enjoy something hearty without feeling deprived.			Easy Pasta with Marinara Sauce (pg. 216) ☐ *Check!*
Week **24**	bringing a mayo-laden dip to a party	bring our Artichoke Spinach Dip Appetizer.			Artichoke Spinach Dip Appetizer (pg. 129) ☐ *Check!*

Week	Instead of	Try This	Date When Completed	Note any positive changes you feel as a result	Recipe to try this week
Week 25	a traditional hamburger	try any of the amazing burger substitutes (read the label to make sure they are vegan, not vegetarian) like MorningStar Farms Veggie Burgers, Gardenburger Black Bean Chipotle Veggie Burger, or Field Roast Hand-Formed Burgers.			Sloppy Janes & Skinny Slaw (pg. 124) ☐ Check!
Week 26	a hot dog	try veggie dogs. You will not know the difference! My favorite brand is Field Roast Vegan Frankfurters. You can also try Yves Veggie Hot Dogs. (By the way, you're halfway through the year! Keep up the good work!)			Field Roast Italian Vegan Sausage & Pepper Sandwich (pg. 112) ☐ Check!
Week 27	a chicken or turkey breast	try Gardein Meatless Chick'n Breasts. Prepared vegan foods are a great way to help transition from eating meat to going vegan, especially if you are still working on your favorite go-to vegan recipe list.			Chick'n Scampi (pg. 224) ☐ Check!
Week 28	making soup with beef or chicken stock	use vegetable stock. You can also use vegetable bouillon cubes instead of animal-based bouillon cubes. I look for brands that are lower in salt. You can always add more salt, if necessary.			Italian Wedding Soup (pg. 143) ☐ Check!

Week	Instead of	Try This	Date When Completed	Note any positive changes you feel as a result	Recipe to try this week
Week 29	putting unhealthy snacks front and center in your fridge	make a big fruit salad and keep it on the top shelf of the fridge in plain sight. You'll be more tempted to snack on it. Use fruits you really enjoy and can't wait to dig into. My favorites are mango and watermelon. I think of these as candy. Look through the produce aisle and choose your favorites so you feel like you're doing something decadent.			Watermelon Quencher (pg. 90) ☐ *Check!*
Week 30	using meat-based spaghetti sauce	choose a quality brand sauce in a jar like tomato & basil or tomato arrabiata for a spicy touch. You can also make a quick marinara sauce and keep extra in the freezer to thaw any time.			Manicotti Florentine with Cashew Ricotta (pg. 206) ☐ *Check!*
Week 31	eating a chicken salad or tuna salad sandwich	make a "chickpea salad" sandwich with mashed chick peas, chopped green onion, vegan mayo, and chopped celery on your favorite vegan bread. Vegenaise Eggless Mayonnaise is a great mayo substitute.			Deli-Style Tuna Salad Sandwich (pg. 130) ☐ *Check!*

Week	Instead of	Try This	Date When Completed	Note any positive changes you feel as a result	Recipe to try this week
Week 32	ordering pizza with everything on it	ask for everything on it except the meat and cheese. It will be loaded with onions, mushrooms, veggies, and will be absolutely delicious. You can order extra sauce to make it zestier. If you are fortunate enough to have a vegan pizza place in your area, enjoy!			Red Pizza (pg. 219) ☐ *Check!*
Week 33	eating bacon or pork products	enjoy Gardein Sweet & Sour Porkless Bites and you'll be in hog heaven. You'll also find that by adding fennel seeds to vegetarian soups or stews, you will get a flavor that you associate with pork because fennel is often added to pork dishes.			Angie's "Pork" Bread (pg. 126) ☐ *Check!*
Week 34	having a steak or chicken breast at a restaurant	order three to four side dishes instead of an entrée. Just ask that they be cooked without butter or milk. To be extra healthy ask for steamed veggies and sprinkle with a little salt and cracked black pepper and fresh lemon. It is likely you will not use as much salt as the chef would if he prepared a typical veggie dish covered in a traditional sauce.			Sweet & Sour Cabbage & "Beef" Soup (pg. 158) ☐ *Check!*

Week	Instead of	Try This	Date When Completed	Note any positive changes you feel as a result	Recipe to try this week
Week **35**	topping your baked potato with butter or sour cream	make fresh salsa your new favorite topping. It's a treat. Check out our Pico de Gallo recipe.			SoCal Street Corn (pg. 227) ☐ *Check!*
Week **36**	butter on your toast	use vegan butter substitutes like Earth Balance Natural Buttery Spread, or use almond butter or avocado. Remember, these still contain fat, so use sparingly. If you buy a good quality bread, you won't need as much spread. I love Ezekiel Sesame Sprouted Grain Bread—hearty and delicious. You can also top with a good quality fruit preserve. Many have no sugar added and eliminate the fat altogether.			Blueberry Banana Muffins (pg. 88) ☐ *Check!*
Week **37**	eating a steak or beef as a main course or part of a salad	try Home-Style Beefless Tips by Gardein. Sauté in a little garlic and olive oil with salt and pepper and you'll find them to be satisfying and protein-rich. Put them in any salad or serve with potatoes and vegetables for a hearty meal. Also, try our recipe for Sweet and Sour Beef and Cabbage Soup. It's so filling and satisfying.			Zucchini Pasta with Lemon Walnut Pesto (pg. 211) ☐ *Check!*

Week	Instead of	Try This	Date When Completed	Note any positive changes you feel as a result	Recipe to try this week
Week **38**	making an omelet or eating eggs for breakfast	make a "nom-lette" —all the omelette ingredients without the eggs or cheese: potatoes, onions, green pepper, topped with avocado and fresh salsa. You won't miss the eggs. This is one of my all-time favorite breakfasts. You can also order this at a restaurant. I use a non-stick pan and just a small drizzle of olive oil for four servings. If you make fresh salsa, it will be so satisfying you won't even miss the eggs.			Italian French Toast (pg. 93) ☐ *Check!*
Week **39**	cake or pie for dessert	opt for fresh berries. You can also sprinkle berries with a little ground flax meal and warm them in a pan. It will taste like pie crust mixed in with the berries, and add some extra fiber to the meal.			Aunt Lena's Blueberry Tarts (pg. 250) ☐ *Check!*
Week **40**	handing out Halloween candy to trick-or-treat visitors	give some favorite vegan candies (candy corn, Twizzlers, Swedish Fish, etc.) and have a few for yourself, but don't eat your entire stash before the kids arrive!			Applesauce Cake with Cinnamon Glaze (pg. 254) ☐ *Check!*

Week	Instead of	Try This	Date When Completed	Note any positive changes you feel as a result	Recipe to try this week
Week 41	making S'mores	make the best vegan s'mores ever by starting with the best vegan marshmallows ever! Sweet & Sara Vegan Marshmallows are the best ever. Use dark chocolate instead of milk chocolate and Nabisco Graham crackers, which are vegan. Do this on special occasions. Sweets are a once in a while pleasure. Otherwise, eat berries to satisfy your sweet tooth.			Rockier Road "Nice" Cream (pg. 259) ☐ Check!
Week 42	scrambling eggs	try Follow Your Heart VeganEgg. This tastes like the real deal and will help you get your egg fix without the cholesterol. It has 40 calories and 1.5 grams of fat per serving.			"Hold the Eggs" Breakfast Scramble (pg. 98) ☐ Check!
Week 43	using eggs as an ingredient in your favorite cake or muffins	make your own flax eggs by mixing 1 tablespoon of flax meal with 3 tablespoons of water for every egg in the recipe. Mix the flax and water and let sit for 20 minutes in the fridge before using. Several recipes in this book use flax eggs. You'll never miss the real egg and will get some extra fiber in your diet.			Pumpkin Muffins with Maple Syrup (pg. 78) ☐ Check!

Week	Instead of	Try This	Date When Completed	Note any positive changes you feel as a result	Recipe to try this week
Week **44**	snacking on yogurt	try yogurt made from coconut or almond milk, like Silk and So Delicious brands, or snack on applesauce. Add a tablespoon of chopped walnuts and some cinnamon if you want to get fancy.			Roasted Beets with Oranges & Macadamia Ricotta (pg. 110) ☐ *Check!*
Week **45**	going to Yelp to find a restaurant	visit www.HappyCow.net to find vegan restaurants worldwide. You'll have fun experimenting with new restaurants and meals at home or while traveling. Your search results will indicate if the restaurant is vegan, vegetarian, or veg-friendly (meaning there are plant-based options).			Pigs in a Blanket (pg. 222) ☐ *Check!*
Week **46**	choosing a fish sandwich or entrée	try Gardein Golden Fishless Filets. They taste like the real thing and get you off the hook.			Corn Thyme Chowder (pg. 152) ☐ *Check!*

Week	Instead of	Try This	Date When Completed	Note any positive changes you feel as a result	Recipe to try this week
Week 47	using a creamy salad dressing	make a quick vegan salad dressing from chapter 11. These are so easy and flavorful, you'll never miss the dairy and your tummy will feel better too. If eating out, ask the waiter to use oil and balsamic vinegar on the salad, or you can just use the vinegar.			Creamy Ranch Dip (pg. 133) ☐ *Check!*
Week 48	gorging on turkey for Thanksgiving dinner	make like the President and give your turkey a pardon. Prepare all the trimmings instead: sweet potatoes, green beans, and mashed potatoes. These dishes will still make it feel like a holiday. You can also use vegan roasts now available during the holidays.			Lentil Shepherd's Pie (pg. 234) ☐ *Check!*

Week	Instead of	Try This	Date When Completed	Note any positive changes you feel as a result	Recipe to try this week
Week 49	having pudding for a snack or dessert	make a great vegan pudding by blending 1 banana, 1 tablespoon of chia seeds, and ½ cup of almond milk in a blender with a few drops of vanilla extract. Let sit in the fridge for 2 hours before serving.			Mom's Chocolate Chip Cookies (pg. 256) ☐ *Check!*
Week 50	your typical sushi order	get a veggie roll, usually offered on almost every sushi menu. They are usually a combination of carrot, daikon, avocado, and asparagus, wrapped in rice and a nori sheet. Get a side order of edamame and you'll get the sushi experience minus the fish.			Orange Ginger "Chicken" Lettuce Wraps (pg. 120) ☐ *Check!*

Week	Instead of	Try This	Date When Completed	Note any positive changes you feel as a result	Recipe to try this week
Week 51	getting a side of Asian-style fried rice which often contains eggs and chicken broth	Choose steamed brown rice. If you're making it at home, sauté in veggie broth, garlic, and a little sesame chili oil. Top with chopped green onion.			Asian Pear, Pink Grapefruit & Avocado Salad (pg. 187) ☐ *Check!*
Week 52	continuing with any animal products you have not yet given up such as lamb, venison, or other foods not mentioned earlier	eliminate them completely. You're almost vegan! Finish the job and enter the New Year as a healthy, trimmer vegan. By the way, no need to have a resolution to lose weight. You've probably already started losing weight naturally because of what you've been doing over the past year. You've done it gradually while developing new habits. That's the best way to keep it off. Use all of the recipes and guidelines in this book to help keep you on track. Congratulations!			Susan's Stuffed Mushrooms with Basil & Walnuts (pg. 118) ☐ *Check!*

CHAPTER 8

Breakfast

"The sixteen hundred dairies in California's Central Valley alone produce more waste than a city of twenty-one million people. That's more than the populations of London, New York, and Chicago combined."
—Gene Baur, activist, author, and president and co-founder of Farm Sanctuary, a farm animal rescue organization.

COCONUT, PECAN & APRICOT GRANOLA

Total Time: 35 minutes   Level: Easy   Serves: 5½ cups

Our friend Melissa loves this crunchy, chewy granola. The best part is the little hint of salt that contrasts with the sweetness of the granola. This is a great recipe for Week 1 (see meal plan on page 57) because it deliciously demonstrates how a good quality granola and nut-based milk far outshines any boxed breakfast cereal with cow's milk.

Ingredients

3 cups rolled oats (not instant)

3 tbsp. coconut sugar or organic cane sugar

½ tsp. salt

⅓ cup agave nectar

4 tbsp. liquid coconut oil

1 tsp. pure vanilla extract

½ cup (approx. 16 pieces) dried apricots, diced

½ cup raw pecans, coarsely chopped

½ cup dried, unsweetened coconut flakes

Silk Coconut Milk or other nut-based milk

Directions

1. Preheat oven to 300°F with rack set in the center of the oven.

2. In a large bowl, mix oats with coconut or cane sugar and salt until thoroughly incorporated. Set aside.

3. Whisk together agave, coconut oil, and vanilla extract, then add to the oat mixture. Mix until oats are thoroughly coated with the agave mixture.

4. Spread mixture into an 11 x 11-inch or other large nonstick baking pan and bake for 15 minutes. Stir thoroughly and bake for another 5 to 10 minutes until mixture is lightly browned. Remove from oven and let cool to room temperature.

5. Add apricots, pecans, and coconut and mix thoroughly.

6. Pour ¾ cup into a bowl with milk as a breakfast cereal. You can also sprinkle it on top of oatmeal or store in plastic bags for a handy snack.

PUMPKIN MUFFINS WITH MAPLE SYRUP

Total Time: 45 minutes   Level: Easy   Serves: 9 muffins

You know it's autumn when pumpkin starts making an appearance in everything from lattes to bagels. A cup of cooked pumpkin contains more than 200 percent of your daily allowance of Vitamin A, great for our vision, and that's great news for our eyes as we enter the second half of life. These taste especially good when they are warm and drizzled with syrup. Try these during Week 7 (see meal plan on page 57) for a satisfying meat-free breakfast.

Ingredients

12-cup muffin tin with paper or foil muffin cups

1½ cups unbleached, all-purpose flour

1 tsp. baking powder

1 tsp. baking soda

½ tsp. salt

1 flax egg*

½ cup canned pumpkin

1 tsp. pure vanilla extract

¾ cup maple syrup, plus extra for serving

2 tbsp. pumpkin seeds, for garnish

Earth Balance Natural Buttery Spread or other vegan buttery spread

1 whole nutmeg

Directions

1. Preheat oven to 375°F. Line the 12-cup muffin tin with 9 muffin cups. The remaining wells will be empty.

2. Mix flour, baking powder, baking soda, and salt in bowl until thoroughly incorporated. Set aside.

---

* Grind whole flax seeds in high speed blender, then measure 1 tbsp. Mix 1 tbsp. of the flax meal with 3 tbsp. water, and chill in fridge for 15 minutes while preparing other ingredients

3. In a separate bowl, mix flax egg, pumpkin, vanilla extract, and maple syrup until thoroughly blended. Slowly add the flour mixture into the wet ingredients until incorporated. Do not overmix.

4. Evenly distribute mixture into nine of the muffin cups. Top each muffin with a few pumpkin seeds. The remaining wells of the pan will remain empty. Bake for 20 minutes.

5. Let muffins cool approximately 10 minutes. Serve with vegan spread and maple syrup while still warm. Use a Microplane or other fine grater to grate a generous sprinkle of the whole nutmeg on the muffins.

CHRISTMAS MUESLI

Total Time: 5 minutes   Level: Easy   Serves: 2

When you can make a crunchy, chewy breakfast cereal from scratch in five minutes, why settle for something out of a box? Rolled oats have a wonderful chewy texture and don't need to be cooked. Experiment using different nuts or dried fruit. This will be a favorite cereal year-round. Week 7 (see meal plan on page 57) is all about healthier breakfasts, and you'll love how easy this one is to assemble. You can also make 3 to 4 times the amount and keep it in the fridge for a ready-to-serve cereal or snack.

Ingredients

1 cup rolled oats, uncooked

¼ cup hazelnuts, chopped

½ cup dried cranberries

2 tbsp. pumpkin seeds

4 tbsp. agave nectar, to taste

2 cups nut-based milk alternative (almond, cashew, coconut)

Directions

1. Mix oats, hazelnuts, cranberries, and pumpkin seeds in bowl. Stir to fully incorporate.

2. Pour mixture into bowls.

3. Drizzle with agave nectar. Add the nut-based milk as you would with any cereal and enjoy.

Tip: Double or triple this recipe and keep in fridge for up to a week for a quick and satisfying breakfast cereal or as an oatmeal topping.

BLUEBERRIES WITH ORANGE CREAM

Total Time: 10 minutes   Serves: 2

Fruit just got sexier. Drizzle a little orange cream on top of blueberries (or any berries) for a sweet and tart treat. If you want something more filling just put the berries and cream on top of oatmeal, a great option for Week 7 (see meal plan on page 57) when you'll be experimenting with meat-free breakfasts.

Ingredients

3 cups blueberries (you can also mix a variety of berries such as blackberries, strawberries, or raspberries)

¼ tsp. grated orange zest

2 tsp. fresh squeezed orange juice

2 tbsp. unsweetened So Delicious Cultured Coconut Milk or other vegan yogurt substitute

1 tbsp. agave nectar

⅛ tsp. pure vanilla extract

2 tbsp. slivered pecans

Directions

1. Separate berries into two serving dishes.

2. Grate the orange zest, then cut the orange in half and squeeze until you have 2 tbsp. of fresh orange juice. Save the remainder of the orange for a snack or smoothie.

3. Mix the orange juice, zest, coconut milk, agave, and vanilla with a wire whisk or fork until thoroughly combined to make orange cream.

4. Drizzle mixture on top of each berry dish.

5. Top with slivered pecans.

OATMEAL
WITH RASPBERRY PURÉE

Total Time: 15 minutes   Level: Easy   Serves: 6 servings

Even something as ordinary as oatmeal can be exciting with the right toppings. Fresh fruit is always best and easiest, but if you want something a little more exciting, you can make this quick raspberry purée in an instant. This recipe is a great option for Week 7 (see meal plan on page 57) when we ask you to consider breakfast without the bacon. You'll find that the high fiber in oatmeal will keep you full and satisfied. The raspberry purée will make it taste like dessert.

Ingredients

6 oz. fresh raspberries, plus extra for garnish

1 tbsp. agave nectar

½ tbsp. lemon juice

4 cups instant oatmeal (or regular oatmeal, if time permits)

½ tsp. salt

7 cups water

fresh mint sprigs, for garnish

Directions

1. Blend raspberries, agave nectar, and lemon juice in a blender or food processor until fully blended to make raspberry purée. Set aside.

2. Mix oatmeal, salt, and water in a glass or other microwaveable bowl. Microwave on high for 60 to 90 seconds or according to package directions. Remove and stir thoroughly.

3. Top with raspberry purée mixture, raspberries, and mint.

BANANA PANCAKES WITH BLUEBERRY BASIL PURÉE

Total Time: 30 minutes   Level: Easy   Serves: 4 servings (8 pancakes)

Blueberry Basil Purée Ingredients

3 cups blueberries

2 tbsp. maple syrup

½ tbsp. lemon juice

3 tbsp. organic brown sugar

small basil leaves, for garnish

organic confectioners' sugar, for garnish

Pancake Ingredients

¾ cup unbleached, all-purpose flour

2 tsp. baking powder

¼ tsp. salt

¾ cups almond or other nut milk

1 flax egg*

3 tbsp. unsweetened apple sauce

small amount of coconut oil

Blueberry Basil Purée Directions

1. Blend 2 cups blueberries, maple syrup, lemon juice, and brown sugar in a blender or food processor until fully blended. This can be made the night before, if desired.

Pancake Directions

1. Using an electric mixer or wire whisk, mix all pancake ingredients, except coconut oil, until fully incorporated.

2. Heat an 11 x 11-inch or other large nonstick pan or griddle and use coconut oil in pan, if necessary. Pancakes will sometimes even stick to nonstick pans.

3. Pour batter into pan ¼ cup at a time. Flip each one when bubbles form on the top of the batter.

4. Drizzle the blueberry purée on the pancakes and garnish with a sprinkle of confectioners' sugar, extra blueberries, and fresh basil leaves.

---

* Grind whole flax seeds in high speed blender, then measure 1 tbsp. Mix 1 tbsp. of the flax meal with 3 tbsp. water, and chill in fridge for 15 minutes while preparing other ingredients.

Pancakes were always a special treat at our house, usually reserved for weekends. The addition of banana makes a moist and sweet batter without the need for eggs. The blueberry basil purée is more sophisticated than the maple syrup we used to enjoy as kids, but you'll love the burst of fresh flavor. Flax eggs, introduced in Week 43 (see meal plan on page 57), are an important part of this recipe and others in this book, helping to bind your ingredients while adding heart-healthy omega-3 fatty acids.

BLUEBERRY BANANA MUFFINS

Total Time: 40 minutes   Level: Easy   Serves: 12 muffins

Blueberry muffins were a favorite at our house for breakfast or a snack. This version is super moist and uses applesauce instead of oil or butter. It's so easy to avoid fat and cholesterol by using plant-based substitutes.

Ingredients

½ cup unbleached, all-purpose flour, plus 1 tbsp. to coat blueberries

1 tsp. baking powder

1 tsp. baking soda

½ tsp. salt

3 ripe mashed bananas

1 flax egg*

¾ cups agave nectar

⅓ cup unsweetened applesauce

1½ cups fresh blueberries

12 paper muffin cups

12-cup muffin pan

Earth Balance Natural Buttery Spread or other vegan buttery spread

Directions

1. Preheat oven to 375°F.

2. Mix 1½ cups flour, baking powder, baking soda, and salt in bowl using a fork or wire whisk until thoroughly incorporated. Set aside.

3. In a separate bowl, mix bananas, flax egg, agave nectar, and applesauce until thoroughly blended. Slowly add in flour mixture until all ingredients are incorporated. Do not overmix.

4. Make sure the blueberries are patted dry to remove any surface moisture. Toss the blueberries gently in approximately 1 tbsp. of flour until lightly coated. This will keep the blueberry color from turning your batter blue. Fold blueberries carefully into the muffin batter.

(Continued)

---

* Grind whole flax seeds in high speed blender, then measure 1 tbsp. Mix 1 tbsp. of the flax meal with 3 tbsp. water, and chill in fridge for 15 minutes while preparing other ingredients.

5. Insert paper cups into a 12-cup muffin pan.

6. Evenly distribute mixture into the cups.

7. Bake for 20 to 25 minutes or until an inserted toothpick comes out clean.

8. Let muffins cool approximately 10 minutes. Serve warm with vegan butter, if desired.

WATERMELON QUENCHER (SANDRA'S FAVORITE SUMMER SMOOTHIE)

Total Time: 5 minutes   Level: Easy   Serves: 1–2

I'm not a morning person and I don't drink coffee, so I have to rely on the goodness of mother nature to wake up each morning. This tastes like a watermelon avalanche—refreshment overload! It will awaken you from the inside out.

Ingredients

1 (approx. 5–6 pounds) miniature seedless watermelon, refrigerated overnight

1 cup frozen mixed berries

3 (2-inch) mint leaves

Directions

1. Scoop out the flesh of the entire watermelon using an ice cream scoop or spoon and place in blender with frozen mixed berries and mint leaves.

2. Blend until fully incorporated.

FUNKY MONKEY SMOOTHIE

Total Time: 5 minutes   Level: Easy   Serves: 1

This is my standard year-round smoothie; it never gets old. With flavors of chocolate, almond butter, and banana, it's hard to go wrong. The rolled oats make it chewy and satisfying. Cacao is the single richest food source of magnesium, which aids in digestion, sleeping, and energy. This will keep you full until lunchtime. You'll want to try this in Week 6 (see meal plan on page 57) when it's time to use vegan chocolate instead of milk chocolate, if you can wait that long. Once you try it, you might find yourself having it a few times a week; it's that good.

Ingredients

1 frozen banana or 1 regular banana with 4 ice cubes

2 tbsp. Ojio Cacao Nibs or 1 tbsp. cacao powder

1 tbsp. almond butter, peanut butter, or other nut butter

¼ cup rolled oats, uncooked (rolled oats do not need to be cooked. Do not substitute with steel cut or Irish oats)

1 tbsp. agave nectar

1 cup cashew milk or other nut-based milk

Directions

1. Mix all ingredients in blender until smooth. You can add more or less almond milk depending on your taste. Use cacao nibs if you like more texture in your shake; use powder for a smoother consistency.

ITALIAN "FRENCH" TOAST

Total Time: 15 minutes   Level: Easy   Serves: 2

Our Italian mother used to make what she called "Italian French Toast" a delicious, savory breakfast treat. She dipped a thick slice of Italian bread into a scrambled egg, fried it in a pan with a little oil, and served it with a sprinkle of salt. It was always a favorite of ours. We were quite surprised to discover that other people added powdered sugar and syrup to their French toast. How strange! We still prefer Mom's Italian version to the sweeter alternative. Here's an even healthier iteration using Follow Your Heart VeganEgg, recommended in Week 42 (see meal plan on page 57).

Ingredients

4 tbsp. Follow Your Heart VeganEgg

1 cup ice cold water

4 (½-inch thick) slices quality, crusty Italian
    bread (stale bread works best)

olive oil spray

salt (regular or Kosher)

Directions

1. Mix the VeganEgg with ice cold water until thoroughly mixed.

2. Dip each slice of bread into the egg mixture until fully soaked with egg mixture.

3. Spray an 11-inch or other large nonstick skillet with olive oil on medium high heat.

4. Fry bread in oil and cook on each side until golden brown.

5. Sprinkle with salt and serve warm.

Avocado on toast is a vegan favorite and the variations are endless. This one has an Italian flair with tomatoes, garlic, and fresh basil. Feel free to experiment with a variety of colors and textures. This is a great recipe for Week 2 (see meal plan on page 57) when you're experimenting with different vegan breads. Ezekiel bread is an excellent choice, especially the sesame seed variety, for extra crunch and texture. It will hold up beautifully with the hearty toppings. Week 36 recommends losing the butter for better bread toppings. We think you'll agree that avocado beats butter all day long.

AVOCADO & TOMATO TOAST

Total Time: 15 minutes   Level: Easy   Serves: 2

Ingredients

4 slices toasted bread (use a quality whole grain bread)

1 tsp. olive oil

1 garlic clove, minced

4 cherry tomatoes, halved

½ avocado, sliced thin

salt and pepper, to taste

2 large basil leaves, rolled and cut into ribbons

microgreens or sprouts, for garnish

Directions

1. Toast bread in oven, toaster, or toaster oven to desired crispness.

2. While bread is toasting, heat olive oil on low to medium heat. Add garlic and sauté until garlic begins to sizzle and become aromatic, about 2 minutes. Add tomatoes and continue to mix with garlic and olive oil for about 3 minutes.

3. Put avocado slices on toast. Sprinkle a little salt and pepper on top.

4. Top generously with tomatoes and basil ribbons.

5. Garnish with microgreens.

LAST MANGO IN PARIS SMOOTHIE

Total Time: 5 minutes   Level: Easy   Serves: 2

This tastes like a smoothie you might order at a spa. The color of the mango and lavender contrast as beautifully as the flavors. It is always ideal to use fresh mango to get the creamy texture but frozen will work in a pinch.

Ingredients

1 cup So Delicious Unsweetened Coconut Milk or other rich nut-based milk, such as cashew

2 cups fresh mango, cubed (if you only have frozen mango, add additional coconut milk and 2–3 tsp. of agave nectar to capture the sweet, creamy texture of fresh mango)

1 frozen banana

½ tsp. vanilla extract

¼ tsp. lavender, for garnish

Directions

1. Mix all ingredients except lavender in blender until smooth.
2. Garnish with lavender.

"HOLD THE EGGS" BREAKFAST SCRAMBLE WITH PICO DE GALLO

Total Time: 15 minutes   Level: Easy   Serves: 2

This recipe is a vegan take on a popular dish in Long Beach, California. It's a Veggie Scramble without the eggs and cheese. The end result is fabulous when served with our fresh classic pico de gallo (salsa) and warm corn tortillas. Week 35 (see meal plan on page 57) recommends using salsa as a low fat topping; when you taste this, you'll want to put it on everything from salads to potatoes. Week 38 recommends losing the eggs. You might ask "what eggs?" after trying this; it's so completely satisfying.

Breakfast Scramble Ingredients

1 cup small red potatoes, quartered

2–3 cups water or enough to cover potatoes while boiling them

salt & pepper, to taste

½ tbsp. oil

½ cup red onion, diced

1 cup button mushrooms, sliced

1 bell pepper, diced

2 cups baby spinach, roughly chopped

1 tomato, diced

2 corn tortillas

Classic Pico de Gallo (recipe below)

½ avocado, sliced

Classic Pico de Gallo Ingredients

1 cup tomatoes, diced

2 tbsp. red onion, diced

1 tbsp. cilantro leaves, tightly packed

1 tbsp. fresh squeezed lime juice

¼ fresh jalapeño pepper, minced, seeds removed

¼ tsp. salt

fresh cracked black pepper, to taste

(Continued)

Breakfast Scramble Directions

1. Place potatoes in cold water and bring to boil. Once boiling, add salt and cook until fork tender, about 12 to 15 minutes.

2. Heat the oil on medium high heat in a nonstick frying pan.

3. Drain the potatoes and cook until browned on the outside. If the mixture gets dry, add a little water.

4. Add onions, mushrooms, and peppers and continue to heat until cooked.

5. Add spinach and tomatoes and cook until spinach is wilted.

6. Place on two serving plates with tortillas and top with Classic Pico de Gallo and diced avocado.

Classic Pico de Gallo Directions

1. Mix all ingredients in a bowl until fully incorporated for a chunky, vibrant topping.

Cupcakes for breakfast? You're not dreaming. Serve these delicious treats without guilt. They contain white beans for extra fiber. But that's not all; the liquid from the bean (also known as aquafaba) serves as an egg substitute and provides unique starch and protein content to this recipe. Once you've enjoyed these treats, you'll be certain that you don't need eggs, butter, and milk to make delicious, light, and moist chocolate cupcakes healthy enough for breakfast.

CHOCOLATE SURPRISE BREAKFAST CUPCAKES

Total Time: 35 minutes   Level: Easy   Serves: 18 cupcakes

Ingredients

1½ cups unbleached, all-purpose flour

1 tsp. baking soda

1 tsp. baking powder

½ tsp. salt

⅓ cup cacao powder or cocoa powder

3 tbsp. aquafaba (liquid from the can of beans)

⅓ cup mashed cannellini beans, rinsed thoroughly

3 ripe bananas

½ cup agave nectar

½ cup organic sugar

⅓ cup Silk Coconut Milk or other nut-based milk

1 tsp. vanilla extract

powdered organic sugar, for garnish

almond milk, to serve with cupcakes

18-cup cupcake tin

18 cupcake papers or foil baking cups

Directions

1. Preheat oven to 375°F.

2. Mix flour, baking soda, baking powder, salt, and cacao powder until incorporated. Set aside.

3. Mix remaining ingredients in a separate bowl with an electric mixer until completely blended. On a low speed, add flour mixture a little at a time until incorporated. Do not overmix.

4. Divide batter equally into 18 muffin cups.

5. Bake for 17 to 19 minutes or until a toothpick piercing the center of a muffin comes out clean.

6. Sprinkle organic powdered sugar on top and serve warm with a glass of almond milk.

INSPIRATIONAL VEGAN

JULIE FEATHERMAN

Founder, Juju Salon & Organics

Beauty without the Beast

The global beauty industry is projected to reach $265 billion by 2017[20]—and that's bad news for animals. Inhumane animal testing is horrific, widespread, and perfectly legal. It's also completely unnecessary.

The FDA doesn't require animal testing, just proof that products are safe.[21] While humane testing options are widely available, many companies aren't using them. Tens of thousands of rabbits, guinea pigs, mice, and rats are killed to test cosmetics in the United States alone.[22] According to People for the Ethical Treatment of Animals, European countries are already moving toward cruelty-free alternatives. "Instead of measuring how long it takes a chemical to burn the cornea of a rabbit's eye, manufacturers can now drop that chemical onto cornea-like 3D tissue structures produced from human cells."[23]. Animals can ultimately be eliminated from

[20] http://www.cosmeticsdesign.com/Market-Trends/Global-beauty-market-to-reach-265-billion-in-2017-due-to-an-increase-in-GDP

[21] http://fashionista.com/2015/01/us-cosmetics-animal-testing-ban

[22] http://www.pcrm.org/research/animaltestalt/cosmetics

[23] http://www.peta.org/issues/animals-used-for-experimentation/cosmetic-household-products-animal-testing/

the product testing equation with ongoing pressure from PETA and other advocacy organizations. In the meantime, a little positive juju couldn't hurt.

Philadelphia Freedom

Nationally renowned Juju Salon & Organics, founded by Julie Featherman, was the first salon in Philadelphia to go cruelty-free. All of Juju's services use cruelty-free and vegan ingredients and products. Julie's mission of liberty and justice for all animals began at age forty-five. Her initial motivation to go vegan stemmed from her concern for the suffering of animals on factory farms. "I was vegetarian forever, still eating dairy," she says. But one day, a vegan friend told her that animals endured even more agony for their milk than those slaughtered for meat. About the same time, Julie read Dr. T. Colin Campbell's *The China Study*[24]. The facts were overwhelming and irrefutable. She made a decision to drop the dairy, and a vegan was born.

Her healthy diet became a launching pad, of sorts. Once Julie went vegan, she was even more motivated to exercise. "I stepped up the workouts to be more well-rounded—strength training, cardio, sculpting, Pilates—I do it all." It's not uncommon for vegan ideals to

spread beyond the dinner plate into other areas of one's life. Julie says, "Evolving to a vegan lifestyle, including vegan clothing and product choices, has strengthened my company's holistic mission."

The salon's location, adjacent to a health food store with a vegan hot bar, was no accident. Julie made a strategic business and health decision that gives her easy access to her favorite foods. "I eat miso, bean or kale soup, lentil patties, tofu, seitan, and collard greens. My husband makes fun of me when I eat my kale burger with salad and chick peas." But Julie takes it in stride because, while she chose to be vegan for the animals, she ultimately reaped the health benefits of a plant-based life. "The impact of this decision has not only improved my weight, energy, and stamina, it has profoundly improved my mood and outlook on life. Health wise, I feel better than I did in my twenties."

Good Fortune, Good Business

The name "Juju" was Julie's childhood nickname, but she also chose it for its Western African meaning—a charm or object designed to bring luck. Her salon has already brought good fortune to animals by offering exclusively cruelty-free products. It also generates happy clients with exciting new brands. Salon patrons quickly learn that

---

[24] https://en.wikipedia.org/wiki/The_China_Study

plant-based products can be quite luxurious, with ingredients like Bulgarian rose water, blood orange, dandelion, grapefruit, and bourbon vanilla. Who couldn't get used to that?

Juju Salon & Organics also carries locally produced Stinky Girl brand body oils and unisex deodorants. Julie's staff is trained in green beauty, organic products, and holistic health and wellness, in addition to cut and color training from top salon academies. She has woven a conscientious thread throughout every area of her business. She's living proof that aligning personal values with one's business model brings consistency, sustainability, and alluring brand appeal.

Not Always Easy Being Green

Julie does have the challenge of sharing a home with a non-vegan family—it's a reality for many vegans who make up only .5 percent of the US population[25]—but challenge is all in a day's work for this honorable entrepreneur. Julie's husband, an omnivore, happens to be a great cook and makes vegan meals for Julie. Julie's daughters, Lucie and Frances, are committed to being lacto-ovo pescetarians, eating dairy, eggs and fish, and are considering

a vegan path. The family does make every effort to be responsible consumers. Julie states, "We make sure that every egg, slice of cheese, fish, or meat that enters our home is USDA organic and raised as humanely as possible, including local dairy milk and cheese and line-caught wild salmon. We try to source from the health food grocer next door, co-ops, and farmers' markets."

It's a scenario faced daily by vegans who live in a home where animal products are in the fridge and on the table and it's not always easy. Julie says "Sometimes my family is eating pizza and I want the carbs, the bread, and the cheese, but I would never trade it in. I'm not going back."

Julie's Tips for Going Vegan After 40: Be Smart, Be Kind

Julie recommends that 40+ vegan wannabes consult with their doctors. "Get bloodwork

[25] http://www.vegetariantimes.com/article/vegetarianism-in-america/

done to gauge where you are. I investigated the best way to eat vegan as a menopausal woman. Your diet may differ depending on your particular health circumstances, hormonal fluctuations, diabetes, etc."

She also recommends being kind to yourself. "If you break your vegan diet, don't be hard on yourself. It's not a cult or a religion—it's a conscious choice you make with every meal. That's been the best way for me to look at it." For Julie, it's not about willpower; it's about conviction. "What stops me from eating animal products is thinking about what happens to the animals. I don't want to participate in that anymore."

Summary: Julie Featherman

Age at Transition to a Vegan Lifestyle: 45

Current Age: 50

Statistics/Changes: "The impact of this decision has not only improved my weight, energy, and stamina, it has profoundly improved my mood and outlook on life. Health wise, I feel better than I did in my twenties."

Original Motivator/Turning Point: Interest in animal welfare; reading *The China Study*

Julie's Tips for Transitioning Vegans Over Age 40:

- Consult your doctor
- Don't be hard on yourself if you break your vegan diet—your next meal is another opportunity to make a conscious, vegan choice

Practical Tips: "Vega bars are great. If I'm at work and I have a million things to do, I'll grab one of their bars. They're high in protein with fruit and almond milk."

What helped Julie ease the transition: Based her food choices on conviction, not willpower.

Questions to Consider

1. If willpower has failed you in your past efforts to eat healthy foods, would having strong convictions about health, animal protection, or saving the environment help you stay the course on a vegan diet?

2. Have you ever broken the rules of any diet, got frustrated, and quit altogether? Would recommitting at every meal help you have long-term success in eating vegan?

3. Do you believe your eating habits are in alignment with your values (e.g., kindness to self, others, love of animals, religious beliefs)?

4. If you plan on going vegan, how will you ensure success if you are living with non-vegans? Would other household members support you in your eating habits?

5. What beauty products do I currently use that are labeled with cruelty-free logos or language?

BONUS RECIPE

JULIE'S FAUX TUNA MEDITERRANEAN SALAD

Salad Ingredients

1 can Sophie's Kitchen Vegan Toona

1 cup chick peas

2 tbsp. capers

½ cup carrots, chopped

2–3 scallion stalks, chopped

handful of Kalamata olives, chopped

Dressing Ingredients

¼ cup balsamic vinegar

2–3 tbsp. olive oil

1 garlic clove, minced

1 tbsp. of caper juice

sea salt & pepper, to taste

Directions

1. Whisk the dressing and fold into the combined salad ingredients.

2. Serve on a bed of mixed greens and sprinkle with freshly chopped mint and a squeeze of lemon juice.

HOW TO KNOW IF A BEAUTY PRODUCT IS CRUELTY-FREE

Symbol or Language Used	What it Means	Who Monitors Compliance?
The Leaping Bunny	This is considered the highest level of cruelty-free products. Companies that use this product must participate in onsite audits and comprehensive compliance standards.	The Coalition for Consumer Information on Cosmetics, which includes eight national animal protection groups.
The PETA Bunny cruelty free	Companies using this symbol have made a pledge to PETA that they will not test on animals or commission others to do so.	People for the Ethical Treatment of Animals
Terms including "Cruelty Free" or "Not Tested on Animals"	Since these terms have not been legally defined they may not mean anything. Their use is unrestricted and may actually be misleading to consumers.	No one. While some of these products may be truly cruelty free, others may not be. It's important to do more investigation of the products. You can download an app called *Is it Vegan?* This allows you to scan a barcode to determine if a product is vegan.

CHAPTER 9
Sandwiches, Sides & Spreads

"I have from an early age abjured the use of meat, and the time will come when men such as I will look upon the murder of animals as they now look upon the murder of men."

—Leonardo da Vinci

ROASTED BEETS WITH BASIL & ORANGE MACADAMIA "RICOTTA"

Total Time: 60 minutes   Level: Medium   Serves: 3–4 side dishes

Grandma's beets never looked or tasted quite like this. Don't be intimidated by roasting beets. These are so easy you'll want to make extra to have on hand.

Roasted Beet Ingredients:

6 medium-sized fresh beets

1 orange,* peeled and sectioned

fresh basil leaves, for garnish

edible flowers or microgreens, for garnish

Beet Vinaigrette Ingredients:

½ cup raw fresh beet, cubed

⅓ cup rice wine vinegar

1 small garlic clove

¼ tsp. salt

fresh ground black pepper

Orange Macadamia Ricotta Ingredients:

½ cup macadamia nuts soaked in water for at least 4 hours or overnight, drained

¼ cup water

½ tsp. fresh orange zest

¼ cup orange juice

½ tbsp. agave nectar

¼ tsp. salt

(Continued)

---

* Cut the wedges by slicing just inside the membrane for a perfect slice, called a "supreme."

110

Directions

1. Preheat oven to 400°F.

2. Cut stems from beets and reserve for another use.*

3. Scrub the beets thoroughly. Wrap each beet loosely in foil while still wet (water will help steam them as they bake) and put on a baking sheet in oven for 50 minutes. While beets are baking, make ricotta (recipe below).

4. Remove beets from oven. When they are cool enough to handle, remove the skins with a paper towel. Cut beets into quarters.

Orange Macadamia Ricotta Directions:

1. Combine the drained macadamia nuts, water, orange zest, juice, agave, and salt in a blender. You can also combine in a tall jar using an immersion blender. Put in fridge while preparing vinaigrette and beets.

Beet Vinaigrette Directions:

1. Using a blender, mix all ingredients until thoroughly combined.

To Serve:

1. Place a scoop of orange macadamia ricotta on the bottom of the plate. Drizzle and splatter the beet vinaigrette around the perimeter of the plate. Place the beets on top of the ricotta.

2. Add orange slices and fresh basil leaves for flavor and appeal. For an added visual, use edible flowers or microgreens.

---

* Stems can be cut and sautéed or put in soups wherever you might use greens.

FIELD ROAST ITALIAN VEGAN SAUSAGE & PEPPER SANDWICH

Total Time: 35 minutes   Level: Easy   Serves: 3–6 servings (1–2 sandwiches per person)

Sausage and pepper sandwiches were always expected at our summer Pennsylvania street fairs. If you learn to make your own roasted peppers as we've outlined below, you'll be hooked. This vegan sausage is also perfect for Week 7 (see meal plan on page 57) when experimenting with new breakfast ideas.

Ingredients

3 red or green bell peppers, halved, stem and seeds discarded

1 package Field Roast Italian Vegan Sausage or other vegan sausage

6 whole grain hot dog buns

chives, for garnish (optional)

Directions

1. Cut peppers in half and roast under broiler until skins are blackened and blistered.

2. Put cooked peppers into a paper bag and roll top of bag down so steam cannot escape. Allow to cool. When peppers have cooled, take out of bag and remove all blistered skin, which should come off easily.

3. Remove plastic casings from sausages. Cut in half down the middle and cook in nonstick pan. Do not add oil or salt. Cook until browned on all sides.

4. Place sausages in buns and top with roasted peppers and chives, if desired.

CREAMY RANCH DIP AND VEGGIE APPETIZER

Total Time: 10 minutes   Level: Easy   Serves: 6–8

This will be your favorite new Ranch dressing. You can also use this in Week 5 (see meal plan on page 57) using it as a substitute for mayo on your sandwich.

Ingredients

1 cup raw cashews soaked in water for at least four hours or overnight, drained

½ cup water

4 tbsp. lemon juice

¼ cup rice wine vinegar

3 tbsp. agave nectar

2 cloves garlic

1 tsp. dry basil

1¼ tsp. salt

4–5 grinds of fresh black pepper

1 tbsp. EVOO

celery sticks, carrot sticks, green onions, for serving

Directions

1. Drain the water from the cashews.

2. Place all ingredients except oil in a blender. Blend until fully incorporated. While still blending, drizzle in oil through top of blender. Continue to mix until dressing is smooth and emulsified.

3. Serve as a dip with celery, carrot sticks, green onions, or any raw vegetable. Add a little nut or coconut milk to thin it out and it's a great salad dressing. Store in squeeze bottle or airtight container in refrigerator for up to one week.

CHESTNUT, FENNEL & AVOCADO CROSTINI WITH ORANGE ESSENCE

Total Time: 20 minutes   Level: Easy   Serves: 4

Fennel is a fresh, crunchy addition to salads, and it pairs well with orange. Because of its high fiber, potassium, and folate, fennel is associated with good heart health. The chestnuts also add a beautiful flavor and texture while being extremely low in fat. This recipe's perfect for Week 2 (see meal plan on page 57) when you'll be trying new vegan breads. You'll find that most baguettes are already vegan, and adding them to your list can bring some variety to your dinner plate.

Ingredients

6 whole chestnuts in shell (use prepackaged shelled chestnuts to save time)

8 (1-inch) slices of French baguette, cut diagonally

1 large avocado

zest of 1 orange

1 tbsp. orange juice

⅓ cup fennel bulb, minced

fennel fronds, for garnish

salt & fresh ground black pepper, to taste

red pepper flakes, to taste

1 cup of grape or cherry tomatoes

(Continued)

Directions

1. If using fresh chestnuts in the shell, place them on a cutting board, flat side down. Using a sharp knife, make a crisscross cut into the top of the chestnut, cutting through the thick shell and slightly into the chestnut meat. If using pre-cooked, shelled chestnuts, dice them and set aside.

2. Place chestnuts on a baking pan underneath the broiler for 5 to 10 minutes, turning periodically for even cooking, until shells begin to open up at the cut seams. Check regularly; if the shells turn black, they have been in the broiler too long. Remove from the oven and place in a paper bag or wrap in a cloth towel. Once cooled, carefully remove shells (they can be sharp). If the chestnut is green or moldy on the inside, discard immediately. Dice the chestnut meat into small pieces.

3. Toast the bread in toaster or oven.

4. Mash the avocado and combine with chestnuts, orange zest, juice, and fennel bulb in a bowl. Add a generous pinch of salt and pepper. Mix thoroughly.

5. Spread the avocado mixture on the toasted bread. Top with fennel fronds and red pepper flakes. Serve with fresh tomatoes.

ITALIAN POTATO SALAD

Total Time: 10 minutes   Level: Easy   Serves: 2

Another recipe born out of the availability of Italian ingredients was this delicious potato salad. While most people think of the heavily laden, mayonnaise-based salad, we make a vinaigrette using olive oil, red wine vinegar, garlic, salt, pepper, and fresh parsley over warm potatoes to put our own spin on this classic dish.

Ingredients

3 cups russet potatoes, large diced

1 tsp. salt

¼ cup red wine vinegar

1 tbsp. EVOO

1 garlic clove, minced

⅛ tsp. fresh ground black pepper

2 tbsp. flat leaf Italian parsley, finely chopped

Directions

1. Put potatoes in cold water. Bring to a boil, add salt, and cook until fork tender, about 10 to 12 minutes.

2. Combine all other ingredients, except parsley, to create vinaigrette.

3. Drain the potatoes and while warm, mix carefully with the vinaigrette. If you like more or less dressing, simply adjust the ingredients, accordingly.

4. Sprinkle chopped Italian parsley on top. Don't worry if the potato slices break apart a bit when mixed or served—this is intended to be a rustic potato salad.

5. Serve warm, room temperature, or cold as a side dish.

Tip: Russet potatoes are dry and will absorb the vinaigrette as they sit.

SUSAN'S STUFFED MUSHROOMS WITH BASIL & WALNUTS

Total Time: 40 minutes   Level: Easy   Serves: 4–6

These bite-sized delights make a wonderful appetizer or side dish.

Ingredients

1 lb. (12–14) large white stuffing mushrooms

¾ cup fresh basil leaves, loosely packed, plus extra for garnish

2 large garlic cloves

¼ cup walnuts

½ cup zucchini, sliced, skin on

2 tbsp. panko breadcrumbs, plus extra for garnish

1 tbsp. lemon juice

1 tbsp. nutritional yeast

Directions

1. Preheat oven to 325°F.

2. Brush any dirt off mushrooms with a damp cloth.

3. Separate stems from caps. Set the mushroom caps aside.

4. Put stems, basil, garlic, walnuts, and zucchini in a food processor. Pulse until coarse.

5. Add breadcrumbs, lemon juice, and nutritional yeast. Pulse again until thoroughly combined.

6. With a teaspoon, fill each cap with a heaping portion of the filling. Place in a baking dish, cover with vented foil, and bake for 25 minutes.

7. Serve warm with lemon wedge. Top with additional breadcrumbs and fresh basil leaves.

Tip: Never soak mushrooms in water; it makes them rubbery and tough.

ORANGE GINGER "CHICKEN" LETTUCE WRAPS

Total Time: 35 minutes   Level: Easy   Serves: 8 wraps (4 people, 2 wraps per person)

Susan and I developed an appreciation for Asian food because it was so different from our usual Italian fare. This dish is very light and satisfying with citrus and ginger flavors and plenty of crunch.

Ingredients

½ tbsp. vegetable oil

1 tsp. Eden Foods Hot Pepper Sesame Oil or other sesame oil

2 green onions, chopped, sliced diagonally

1 large garlic clove, minced

⅓ cup orange juice

Gardein Teriyaki Chick'n Strips, small diced (discard sauce pouch)

1 can water chestnuts, drained, diced small

zest of 1 large orange

1 tsp. fresh grated ginger

1 tbsp. soy sauce or tamari

½ tbsp. black sesame seeds

1 head butter lettuce, leaves separated, rinsed and patted dry

Toppings

black sesame seeds

shredded carrots

mung bean sprouts

fresh cilantro, chopped

green onion, sliced diagonally

fresh cilantro, chopped

chopped cashews

orange wedges (optional)

(Continued)

Directions

1. Heat vegetable oil and sesame oil in large pan on medium low heat.

2. Add the green onion and garlic and sauté until vegetables get soft, about 2 minutes.

3. Add the orange juice and stir an additional minute.

4. Add the chicken and water chestnuts. Stir thoroughly for another minute

5. Remove the pan from heat. Mix in orange zest, ginger, soy sauce, and black sesame seeds. Mix until thoroughly combined.

6. Separate mixture into four portions and serve each portion with 3–4 butter lettuce leaves.

7. Let each individual top with their favorite toppings. Serve with orange wedges, if desired.

Tip: The cheese, provided by Field Roast brand, is as creamy as we remember and perfect for Week 15 (see meal plan on page 57) when choosing cheese substitutes or Week 18 as a substitute for your typical fast food burger or sandwich. The longer the salad sits, the better the hoagie. You'll never throw away leftover salad again.

ITALIAN SALAD HOAGIES

Total Time: 15 minutes   Level: Easy   Serves: 2–4 (or 1 hungry junior high school student)

This dish might only be fully understood by Wyoming Area Junior High School, where the Salad Hoagie used to be the best thirty-five cents you could spend. (The cheese was ten cents extra.) What made it so good was that the rolls were baked fresh every day. As we poured out of school and headed for the store, employees would fill the warm bread with salad that was marinating in Italian dressing and layer in some creamy American cheese. Susan and I would each eat a foot-long portion and never worry about overdoing the carbs.

Ingredients

2 slices Vegan Chao Cheese Slices by Field Roast or other vegan cheese substitute

1 cup romaine lettuce, chopped into bite sized pieces

1 cup cucumber, sliced, quartered

¼ cup tomato, diced

¼ cup red onion, sliced

1 tsp. olive oil

3 tbsp. balsamic vinegar

salt & pepper, to taste

1 (12-inch) hoagie roll or submarine sandwich roll

pepperoncini, for garnish

Directions

1. Mix the lettuce, cucumber, tomato, onion, oil, vinegar, salt, and pepper in a bowl. (this tastes even better if the mixed salad sits a few hours)

2. Place the vegan cheese inside each roll.

3. Top with salad.

SLOPPY JANES & SKINNY SLAW

Total Time: 45 minutes   Level: Easy   Serves: 5

Skinny Slaw Ingredients

2 cups finely sliced green cabbage

2 cups finely sliced red cabbage

1 cup red onion, finely sliced

1 cup carrot, finely julienned

1 cup (1 bunch) chopped fresh cilantro, stems discarded

juice of 1 lime

½ tbsp. celery seeds

1 tbsp. agave nectar

salt and fresh cracked black pepper, to taste

Sloppy Jane Ingredients

1 tsp. olive oil

1½ cups red bell pepper, stem and seeds removed and discarded, diced small

1½ cups leek, minced, white part only

4 cups Beefy Crumbles by Beyond Meat

¼ tsp. garlic powder

3 tbsp. organic brown sugar

1 cup Annie's Naturals Organic Ketchup

2 tbsp. balsamic vinegar

¾ tbsp. salt

fresh ground black pepper, to taste

5 vegan rolls

Skinny Slaw Directions

1. Mix all slaw ingredients and set aside.

Sloppy Jane Directions

2. Heat oil in frying pan. Add red pepper and leek, and sauté until softened, 3 to 5 minutes. Add remaining ingredients and cook on low to medium heat until fully incorporated and warm.

3. Place the mixture on top of the rolls. Top with a generous portion of slaw.

Slightly more sophisticated than the Sloppy Joe, the Jane uses balsamic vinegar and leeks for a mild yet zesty flavor. The slaw adds a beautiful contrast with color, crunch, and fiber. Reach for this recipe in Week 14 (see meal plan on page 57) when you want your beef fix without the fat and cholesterol. This satisfies the heartiest of appetites.

ANGIE'S "PORK" BREAD

Total Time: 45 minutes   Level: Medium   Serves: 6

Pork Bread was a family treat whenever our mother made it. We initially became introduced to this recipe by Grandma Maira, who called it "Umbrialatta." The aroma of garlic powder and onions enrobed in that toasting, sesame seed–covered dough wafting from the oven made this a meal that enticed everyone within smelling distance! Our mother often served this scrumptious bread along with one of her homemade soups, and always made a little extra for lunches the next day. Beware: it's addictive!

Ingredients

½ package of Trader Joe's Pizza Dough or other vegan pizza dough

3 links Field Roast Italian Vegan Sausages, room temperature

olive oil spray

1 tbsp. toasted sesame seeds

1 (24 oz.) jar Barilla Tomato & Basil Sauce or our homemade marinara sauce recipe (page 216)

Directions

1. Shape dough into the size of a baseball and roll on a floured surface such as a cutting board or large table, to about ⅛-inch thickness in a rectangular shape.

2. Remove the plastic casing from the sausages and cut into tiny crumbles with a knife or food processor.

3. Spread crumbles on the dough evenly, covering as much of the surface as possible, all the way to the ends.

4. Start rolling the dough from the longer side toward the opposite side, just like you would if you were making cinnamon rolls. Keep the roll fairly tight and when you reach the end, seal the edge of the flap onto the long cylinder you have just formed. Then bring the two ends of the cylinder together to form a ring.

(Continued)

5. Spray the cylinder with olive oil spray and sprinkle with the sesame seeds. Press the seeds lightly into the dough to keep them from falling off.

6. Bake on the middle rack for 20 minutes until the top starts to brown. Cut into 6 equal wedges and serve each wedge with ½ cup of heated marinara sauce.

If you've ever ordered the cheesy artichoke spinach dip appetizer served warm with tortilla chips at a restaurant, you will understand the allure of this dish. The cholesterol is gone thanks to the use of nuts and nutritional yeast. You can make it even higher in fiber by serving it with carrots, celery, or cucumber slices. Week 24 (see meal plan on page 57) will give you a reason to try this, but be warned, once you bring it to your favorite potluck you'll be expected to make it again and again.

ARTICHOKE SPINACH DIP APPETIZER

Total Time: 40 minutes*   Level: Easy   Serves: 6–8 servings

Ingredients

2 (14 oz.) cans Native Forest Quartered Artichoke Hearts

1 cup cashews (soaked in water in fridge at least 4 hours or overnight, drained)

1 cup water

2 cloves garlic, peeled and minced

3 tbsp. nutritional yeast

1 tbsp. lemon juice

1 tsp. salt

1 cup frozen spinach, cooked

¼ cup panko breadcrumbs

olive oil spray

blue corn or traditional tortilla chips

Directions

1. Preheat oven to 350°F.

2. Drain one can of artichoke hearts with strainer and rinse thoroughly with water. Blend in high speed blender with cashews, water, garlic, nutritional yeast, lemon juice, and salt until smooth and creamy. Place mixture in mixing bowl and set aside.

3. Drain the second can of artichoke hearts with strainer and rinse thoroughly with water. Chop into small ¼-inch cubes.

4. Squeeze excess water from cooked spinach. Add spinach and chopped artichoke hearts to cashew mixture and stir thoroughly.

5. Place mixture in baking dish and spread evenly to edges of dish. Evenly distribute breadcrumbs on top of mixture. Spray lightly with olive oil.

6. Bake uncovered for 20 minutes.

7. Serve warmed mixture immediately with tortilla chips or fresh vegetables.

---

* Cashews must be soaked at least 4 hours or overnight prior to preparing.

DELI-STYLE TUNA SALAD SANDWICH

Total Time: 20 minutes*   Level: Easy   Serves: 3

Tuna sandwiches were a lunch staple at our house. This new classic version uses a quick, homemade oil and egg-free mayonnaise that has only four ingredients. It's better than any jarred mayo available and the sandwich is a convincing imposter for the classic tuna salad that we enjoyed as kids. Whichever week you're on, you'll love this sandwich and find countless ways to use the homemade mayo recipe; it's quick and easy and made from delicious cashews.

Deli Style Tuna Salad Ingredients

1 (15 oz.) can chickpeas, drained (save the chickpea liquid for aquafaba)

4 tsp. Best Vegan Mayo

1 tbsp. capers, drained

1 celery stalk, small diced

½ tsp. salt

fresh ground black pepper, to taste

6 slices whole grain vegan bread

Best Vegan Mayo Ingredients

1 cup cashews (soaked in water in fridge at least 4 hours or overnight, drained)

1 garlic clove

2 tsp. apple cider vinegar

½ tsp. sea salt

---

* Cashews must be soaked at least 4 hours or overnight prior to preparing.

Deli-Style Tuna Salad Sandwich Directions

1. Mix chickpeas, Vegan Mayo, and capers in food processor until mostly smooth, resembling tuna fish.

2. In a mixing bowl, combine chickpea mixture with celery, salt, and pepper and stir until thoroughly combined.

3. Spread mixture onto three slices of bread. Top with the remaining slices. Serve with tomato or pickles.

Best Vegan Mayo Directions

1. Blend all mayo ingredients until smooth and creamy.

2. Makes approximately ¾ cup mayo, more than needed for this recipe. Keep the remaining mayo in fridge for up to 3 days.

ZUCCHINI FRIES WITH RANCH DRESSING

Total Time: 30 minutes   Level: Easy   Serves: 4 (makes about 2 dozen fries)

Meet your new favorite fry, baked without potatoes or oil—just crunch and flavor for kids of all ages!

Ingredients

¼ cup unbleached, all-purpose flour

½ tbsp. sea salt, plus extra for seasoning

5–6 grinds of fresh ground black pepper

½ tsp. sweet paprika

½ cup aquafaba (liquid from the can of beans)

⅓ cup panko breadcrumbs

⅓ cup nutritional yeast

1 lb. (2 medium-sized) zucchini

Creamy Ranch Dip (page 113) or quality ketchup

Directions

1. Preheat oven to 425°F.

2. Mix flour, salt, pepper, and paprika in a bowl. Set aside.

3. Place the aquafaba in a separate bowl. Set aside.

4. Combine breadcrumbs and nutritional yeast in a third bowl.

5. Cut the rounded ends off the zucchini. Cut into "fries" about ½ inch in thickness and 3 to 4 inches in length depending on the size of the zucchini.

6. Coat one fry in flour. Shake off excess flour. Dip into aquafaba. Then dip into breadcrumb bowl. Place fry on rack. Repeat with remaining fries.

7. Bake on a wire rack on top of a baking sheet. Cook for 15 to 17 minutes or until brown and crispy.

8. Remove from oven. Sprinkle with additional salt, pepper, and paprika. Serve with Creamy Ranch Dip/Dressing or ketchup.

INSPIRATIONAL VEGAN

TOM NOWAK

Financial Planner

Tom before going vegan

A slimmer, healthier Tom on a plant-based diet

A Balanced Portfolio

Illinois-based scientist turned financial planner Tom Nowak made the transition to a vegan lifestyle well after the age of forty. He said "I was moving away from red meat and trying to be more of a vegetarian for some time but there was a trigger that gave me the incentive to try it at age sixty."

Tom had been holding on to a prescription for statin drugs given to him by his doctor; he was reluctant to fill it. As a former scientist for a large drug manufacturer, he knew about the risks associated with statins, including the risk of Type 2 diabetes. Fortunately, a chance encounter with an old friend presented him with a medication-free alternative. Tom would soon learn that the best treatment for his high cholesterol was not at the pharmacy, but at the grocery store.

The Ultimate Prescription

"I ran into a friend who I had not seen in a long time. He lost a lot of weight and I was a little surprised to see that he changed so dramatically. He was not too far from my age. We began to talk about health issues." Tom told his friend about the statin prescription from his doctor. His friend offered a simple suggestion: read *The China Study*, a book by Dr. T. Colin Campbell. It was an ideal recommendation for someone of Tom's scientific background. Written by a medical doctor, *The China Study* outlines what is perhaps the most compelling and thorough longitudinal case study in support of health and longevity through veganism.

Tom said, "The book gave me the incentive to tell my doctor I was going to try a vegan diet instead of going on the statin drug." Tom agreed to go back for follow-up visits with his doctor. At his six-week visit, Tom's cholesterol, weight, and blood pressure dropped. After an additional six weeks, the doctor said there was no need to take the statin drugs. In six months, Tom had lost between fifteen to twenty pounds. He admits the weight drop to 175 pounds happened so fast that his wife laughed at how his clothes looked on him. "It was so gratifying going through the closet and saying 'we won't need these clothes anymore.'" It's not surprising that his wife joined him in this new way of eating. Tom was a shining example of the profound impact of a plant-based lifestyle.

Living by the Numbers

But that was just the beginning. His cholesterol, which had been moving into the 220–230 range, was now stabilized at 180. The doctor, who had also recommended an ace inhibitor, a vasodilator that reduces high blood pressure, told Tom he no longer needed the drug after going vegan—his blood pressure was just right for his age. On Tom's second trip back to the doctor, the nurse asked, "What was the name of that book you were reading?"

In addition to the numerical changes in Tom's chart, there were other changes that defied measurement. "Weight loss improved my health so much, it encouraged me to exercise more. I went from one day to two days a week to my yoga class and I feel better than I did in my twenties in so many ways. I've had back issues since my twenties but I was recently using a snow blower at my home in the Chicago area and, normally, I would feel like I need to be in traction afterwards." But this time, he didn't feel any pain after using the snow blower. "I felt like a million bucks," he added. After seeing and feeling the dramatic results of the change, Tom admitted "I still kind of wish I got the memo years ago."

Don't we all? When results are significant and life altering, it can make us wonder why we took so long to make a change. But most of us often don't make changes until something gets our attention in a big way: a doctor's visit, a health scare, something that urgently awakens us from what Tom calls a state of being "comfortably unaware," a reference to a book of the same name by Dr. Richard Oppenlander.

Food for Thought

Tom increased his own awareness by educating himself on all aspects of the vegan lifestyle: by reading articles and watching documentaries like *Cowspiracy* and *Forks Over Knives*, and reading books by Dr. John McDougal, an advocate of low-fat vegan diets.

With his commitment to learning more, Tom discovered more than just the health benefits of veganism. He also learned about the horrific animal suffering on factory farms and the negative environmental consequences that happen as a result of mass meat and dairy production and consumption. While these weren't the reasons that prompted him to become vegan in the first place, he calls them "strong triggers to keep him from turning back."

Value Added

Why is it that in the second half of our lives, our values seem to push their way to the forefront? They were with us all along, but often after forty, something shifts. Whether it's because we are trying to impart these values on our children as they emerge into adulthood, or simply trying to fill a need for simplicity in our lives, there seems to be more of a focus on aligning our ethics, our careers, and our legacies. We often take a mental inventory of the various parts of our lives and more readily notice when something just doesn't fit. Tom found a way to bring that alignment into being when he transitioned into financial planning eleven years ago.

Today, at age sixty-three and still committed to a vegan diet, Tom wrote two books: *Low Fee Socially Responsible Investing: Investing in Your Worldview On Your Terms* and *Low Fee Vegan Investing: Taking Veganism to the Next Level*. The books help readers align their values with their investments. (These were exciting reads for me—especially when I discovered that my own financial planner had invested a portion of my money in a fund that included McDonald's Corporation—horrors!) As it turns out, good values make for good investment decisions. Many socially responsible funds are showing healthy returns for people and the planet.

Investing in Your Future

Tom also knows that world trends change and so should investment strategies. "What's happening with investments today is like what happened with fossil fuels—at one point, they weren't a great place to be. Owning a diversified mix of large company stocks that are more representative of the post-fossil-fuel age economy may result in wiser investment opportunities."

The next shift will happen when there is a price increase on carbon. Tom says, "Meat and dairy will cost so much more that people will start eating vegan, and it's going to hurt those stocks. You can preemptively avoid those stocks in your portfolio, if not for moral reasons, then because it will make good financial sense." Tom adds, "The average person doesn't look at their portfolio. There are meat and dairy companies galore. That is just part of the index, part of the benchmark. In the area of sustainable investing, believe it or not, there is no one that's ever put together a vegan or vegetarian mutual fund. That's the reason I wrote the books. I've met with advisors in different parts of the country based on my travels. I've developed something that could be the basis for a broad number of financial products for people in different price points. I would like a low-cost mutual fund that people can access through their regular brokerage firm. As a one-person shop, I can't support it, but there are others that are watching this very carefully; a couple of fund managers whose fellow colleagues collectively manage billion-dollar funds are watching what I'm doing and may be in the position to put together a fund to serve the vegan community at large. That would be a dream come true for me—it solves animal cruelty and medical and environmental problems."

If aging well brings with it the desire to align robust health, an environment of kindness to all living things, and a sustainable planet, it sounds like Tom is developing the perfectly balanced portfolio—a teachable moment for us all.

Summary: Tom Nowak
Age of Change to Veganism: 60
Current Age: 63
Statistics/Changes:

- Weight: 200 to 174
- Cholesterol: 200–230 reduced to 180
- BP: High to Normal Range
- No need to take statin drugs or ace inhibitors initially prescribed by doctor

Original Motivator/Turning Point:

- Desire to avoid statin drugs
- Reading *The China Study*, by T. Colin Campbell, MD
- Witnessing dramatic weight loss of another person who went vegan

Tom's Tips to Those Trying Vegan Over Age 40:

- Stick with it—don't give up while your body is adjusting.
- There could be some stomach distress due to more fiber, or you might just have an intolerance to gluten or some of the foods you are eating.
- It's becoming easier to stay on a vegan diet because it's more mainstream.
- Don't worry about what others say—think about what your doctor will say.
- Keeping it simple is not a bad thing.

Practical Tips:

- Add simple starches like rice and potatoes as the main course with vegetables on the side.

What Helped Ease the Transition:

- Coconut-based ice creams
- Happy Cow app to find vegan restaurants

Questions to Consider:

1. How receptive would your doctor be if you spoke with him or her about a plant-based diet? What, if any, prescriptions might be ultimately eliminated if you made dietary changes?
2. Have you had any health conditions or health scares that made you consider a change in diet and lifestyle? What changes were you able to make and keep?
3. Do you find that after the age of forty, you are drawn to more simplicity in your lifestyle, diet, time management, or living space? What changes have you made to create a simpler life?

4. Do you feel that all areas of your life are in balance or alignment (e.g., values, diet, financial investments, career)? Would you make any changes or adjustments to achieve more congruity in your life?

CHAPTER 10

Soups & Stews

"Plant-based eating is recognized as not only nutritionally sufficient but also as a way to reduce the risk for many chronic illnesses."
—*Becoming a Vegetarian*, Harvard Medical School

ITALIAN WEDDING SOUP

Total Time: 30 minutes   Level: Easy   Serves: 4–6

This soup and this entire chapter will be your best reference for Week 28 (see meal plan on page 57) as you discover that vegetable broth brings fresh, satisfying, and cholesterol-free flavor to any soup.

Ingredients

2 celery stalks, diced

1 cup white onion, diced

1 large carrot, diced

1 tbsp. olive oil

8 cups vegetable broth

¾ cup acini de pepe pasta or Israeli couscous

1 package Field Roast Italian Vegan Sausages, cases removed, sliced at angle or diced

2 cups baby spinach leaves, stems removed, loosely packed

Go Veggie! Grated Parmesan Style Topping or other vegan Parmesan cheese, for garnish

Directions

1. Sauté celery, onion, and carrot in 1 tbsp. olive oil until softened, 3–5 minutes.

2. Add broth and bring to boil.

3. Add pasta and reduce heat to medium. Cook according to package directions (about 8 minutes).

4. When pasta is cooked, add sausage slices and spinach and stir until wilted, a few minutes. Sausage slices should be heated through and do not have to be cooked.

5. Serve immediately and garnish with vegan Parmesan cheese.

GARLIC LEMON BISQUE WITH SRIRACHA KALE CHIP GARNISH

Total Time: 50 minutes   Level: Medium   Serves: 4–6

This bisque gets its creaminess from cannellini beans, a staple in any Italian household.

Garlic Lemon Bisque Ingredients

3 tbsp. minced garlic

½ cup minced shallots

½ tbsp. EVOO

2 (15 oz.) cans cannellini beans

3 cups low-sodium vegetable broth

zest of 1 lemon, plus extra for garnish

3 tbsp. (1 medium lemon) lemon juice

1 tsp. salt

fresh ground black pepper, to taste

Sriracha Kale Chip Garnish Ingredients

1 tsp. olive oil

large pinch salt

several grinds of fresh ground black pepper

1 tsp. agave

½ tsp. Tapatio Salsa Picante Hot Sauce

4 large kale leaves, including stems

1 tbsp. nutritional yeast

Directions

1. Sauté minced garlic and shallot in olive oil for 3 minutes until vegetables are soft.

2. Add beans and broth. Bring to boil.

3. Reduce heat and simmer for 20 minutes.

4. Using an immersion blender or regular blender, purée the soup until creamy.

5. Add lemon zest, juice, salt, and pepper to soup. Stir to fully incorporate.

6. Top with sriracha kale chips, additional lemon zest, and fresh cracked pepper.

(Continued)

Sriracha Kale Chip Garnish Directions

1. Preheat oven to 350°F.

2. In a bowl, mix olive oil, salt, pepper, agave, and hot sauce until combined.

3. Wipe all moisture off of kale leaves with paper towel until they are completely dry—this is key to creating crispy kale. A salad spinner is also helpful to remove excess water. Cut out the stem and cut or tear the remaining leaves in half.

4. Put kale leaves on a baking sheet and brush with the olive oil mixture. Leave room between the leaves to allow them to get crispy instead of just baking. Sprinkle with nutritional yeast.

5. Bake for 15 minutes. Check them after 12 minutes to make sure they are not burning. Use as garnish for soup.

ANGIE'S SWISS CHARD AND CHICK PEA SOUP

Total Time: 45 minutes   Level: Easy   Serves: 6

Our mother used to make this hearty soup that provides more than 600 percent of your daily allowance of Vitamin K, which is linked to bone health—especially important for women over age forty.

Ingredients

1 bunch Swiss chard

1 tbsp. olive oil

1 cup onion, finely diced

2 cloves of garlic, finely diced

9 cups water

8 oz. of Hunt's Tomato Sauce

1 tbsp. salt

1 can chickpeas (drain and reserve the liquid or "aquafaba")

fresh cracked ground pepper

red pepper flakes

flat leaf Italian parsley leaves

lemon wedges (optional)

crusty Italian bread

Directions

1. Remove leaves from the stems of the chard. Cut the leaves in strips.

2. With a potato peeler, remove some of the outer surface of the stems (They can be tough, but are very flavorful, so this is worth a little effort.) Dice the stems in small pieces.

3. Over medium heat, add olive oil, diced stems, and onion to a soup pot. Sauté until transparent. Reduce heat. Add garlic and Swiss chard leaves, sauté for 1 additional minute. (Be careful not to brown or burn the garlic as it will become bitter.)

4. Add the water, tomato sauce, salt, and chickpeas. Simmer for 1 hour.

5. Serve with fresh cracked pepper and red pepper flakes if you like a little extra heat.

6. Top with fresh flat leaf Italian parsley. A fresh squeeze of lemon is another option that brightens up the flavor. Serve with crusty Italian bread for a real treat!

CLASSIC TOMATO BASIL SOUP

Total Time: 30 minutes   Level: Easy   Serves: 4

Tomatoes are plentiful in Italian households. This soup is great any time of year but is especially good during the fall and winter months. Serve with crusty bread and a green salad for a satisfying lunch or dinner.

Ingredients

2 tbsp. fresh garlic cloves, minced

2 tbsp. olive oil

1 (28 oz.) can Muir Glen Organic Tomato Sauce or your favorite organic tomato sauce

1 tbsp. dried basil

1 tsp. salt

1–2 pinches red pepper flakes

¾ cup almond milk or other nut milk

2 tbsp. fresh basil leaves, tightly packed, plus extra for garnish

1½ tsp. agave nectar

5 grinds of fresh black pepper

6 tbsp. panko breadcrumbs, for garnish

Directions

1. Sauté garlic and olive oil in nonstick soup pot until garlic starts to warm and become aromatic, about 1–2 minutes. Be careful not to burn garlic.
2. Add tomato sauce, dried basil, salt, and red pepper flakes and bring to boil.
3. Reduce heat and simmer 10 minutes.
4. Put contents of saucepan into a blender and add almond milk, fresh basil leaves, and agave. Blend until smooth.
5. Return to heat to warm up thoroughly. Add pepper to taste.
6. Ladle into bowls and garnish with panko breadcrumbs and additional basil leaves.

THAI COCONUT SOUP WITH LIME & CILANTRO

Total Time: 45 minutes   Level: Easy   Serves: 6–8

This soup gets its creaminess from coconut milk and cauliflower. It takes a humble vegetable that we grew up eating and adds a burst of Thai flavor. It's rich so a little goes a long way. Serve with lots of fresh cilantro, dried, unsweetened coconut, and lime wedges.

Ingredients

1 tbsp. Earth Balance Natural Buttery Spread or other vegan butter

½ tbsp. olive oil

5½ cups (1 average sized) cauliflower, stems discarded, small diced

1¼ cups (1 large) leek, white part only, finely chopped

1 carrot, diced

1 tbsp. dried coriander

3 cups low-sodium vegetable broth

1 cup Native Forest Organic Classic Coconut Milk or Thai Kitchen Pure Coconut Milk

fresh cilantro, for garnish

dried, unsweetened coconut flakes, for garnish

lime wedges, for garnish

several grinds of fresh black pepper, for garnish

Directions

1. Melt the buttery spread and olive oil in a sauce pan on medium heat.
2. Add the cauliflower, leek, carrot and sauté until tender, about 5 minutes. Stir regularly to prevent sticking or burning. Reduce heat if mixture starts to burn.
3. Add the coriander and vegetable broth.
4. Bring to a boil, then reduce the heat to low and simmer for 20 minutes until vegetables are soft.
5. Remove from heat. Blend the soup while in the pot with an immersion blender or pour into a standard blender and purée until smooth.

(Continued)

6. Pour back into the pot.

7. Shake the can of coconut milk thoroughly. Then pour 1 cup into the soup. Mix until fully incorporated.

8. Serve with fresh cilantro, dried coconut flakes, lime wedges, and fresh cracked black pepper.

CORN THYME CHOWDER

Total Time: 35 minutes   Level: Easy   Serves: 4

Our dad loved fresh picked corn. It wasn't a Pennsylvania summer without it. This is a perfect example of a soup recipe from Week 9 (see meal plan on page 57) where much of the creaminess comes from puréeing the vegetables instead of using heavy cream.

Ingredients

1 tbsp. Earth Balance Natural Buttery Spread

½ tbsp. olive oil

1 cup white onion, small diced

1 carrot, small diced

1 celery rib, small diced

1 garlic clove, minced

3½ cups fresh corn kernels, cut off the cob

3 cups vegetable broth

1 cup cashew milk

½ tsp. dried thyme

1 tbsp. fresh lemon juice

fresh thyme, for garnish

Directions

1. Heat the buttery spread and olive oil over medium heat until melted.

2. Add onion, carrot, celery, and garlic and sauté until vegetables are softened, about 10 minutes. If it gets too dry, add a little vegetable broth.

3. Add corn, broth, milk, and thyme. Cook for an additional 10 minutes uncovered at a slow boil.

4. Using an immersion blender, blend the soup until it is creamy but still has texture. Or you can take half the soup mixture and blend in a traditional blender, then pour it back into the pot.

5. Add lemon juice and mix.

6. Ladle into bowls and garnish with fresh thyme, if desired.

ANTIOXIDANT SOUP

Total Time: 30 minutes   Level: Easy   Serves: 4

A local California restaurant serves a flavorful, rich soup that is dark green and loaded with kale, spinach, and other great veggies. Here's our rendition of that same soup and it's got Week 9 (see meal plan on page 57) written all over it. The purée, which includes sweet potatoes, is so sweet, creamy, and delicious that even your biggest kale-phobic family members will love it.

Ingredients

2 cups sweet potatoes, peeled, cubed

1 cup red onion, chopped

1 garlic clove

5 stems thyme

2 cups canned tomato sauce

6 cups vegetable broth

6 cups kale leaves, stems removed

lemon wedges, for garnish

shelled pumpkin seeds, warmed in a pan until brown, for garnish

fresh basil leaves, for garnish

dried red pepper flakes, for garnish

Directions

1. Put all soup ingredients in pot and bring to boil.
2. Simmer for 20 minutes
3. Put soup in blender and purée.
4. Ladle into bowls and garnish with a squeeze of lemon, warmed pumpkin seeds, and fresh basil leaves. Add red pepper flakes if you like a little heat.

JACKFRUIT CHILI

Total Time: 30 minutes   Level: Medium   Serves: 4 servings

Jackfruit has the texture of shredded meat and takes on the flavor of the chili ingredients. This is one recipe where it is preferable to used canned fruit. Fresh jackfruit is too sweet for this savory meal.

Jackfruit Chili Ingredients

2 (14 oz.) Native Forest Organic Jackfruit

1 cup onion, chopped

1 tbsp. olive oil

2 garlic cloves, minced

2 tbsp. chili powder

2 tsp. cumin

1 tsp. ground coriander

4 tbsp. agave nectar

salt, to taste

1 (28 oz.) can Muir Glen Organic Tomato Sauce

5-6 grinds fresh black pepper

Tortilla Topping (recipe to follow)

cilantro, chopped

green, red, or white onion, chopped

vegan sour cream, for garnish

Tortilla Topping Ingredients

1 corn tortilla

½ tbsp. olive oil

pinch of paprika

pinch of salt

Directions

1. Drain the jackfruit in a strainer and rinse thoroughly

2. On low to medium heat sauté chopped onion with oil until softened and translucent, about 5 minutes.

3. Add jackfruit and break it up with wooden spoon or spatula until it is in shreds. It will look like shredded pork when thoroughly broken up. Continue to stir and break up the fruit for another 5 minutes.

(Continued)

156

4. Add minced garlic, and remainder of ingredients and stir thoroughly. Let simmer for another 10 minutes, stirring occasionally.

5. Pour chili into bowls. Add tortilla topping (recipe below), cilantro, and onion. Garnish with sour cream, if desired.

Tortilla Topping Directions

1. Cut the tortilla into thin shreds about 2 inches long.

2. Heat olive oil in nonstick pan on medium heat. Add tortilla shreds, a pinch of salt, and paprika to add color and flavor.

3. Continue to cook until the tortilla shreds are crispy, about 5 minutes. Set aside.

SWEET & SOUR CABBAGE & "BEEF" SOUP

Total Time: 45 minutes   Level: Easy   Serves: 6–8 bowls of soup

Our good friend Michael grew up eating sweet and sour soup made with cabbage and beef. This soup tastes just like the original but uses Home-Style Beefless Tips by Gardein instead of beef. The texture of these beefy chunks will fool you. This is a perfect soup when you're craving something hearty and meaty. It's filling and satisfying any time of year. You'll especially enjoy it in Week 14 (see meal plan on page 57) when looking for a satisfying beef substitute; this soup delivers the goods!

Ingredients

2 bags Home-Style Beefless Tips by Gardein

1 tbsp. olive oil

1 cup yellow onion, chopped

2 cloves of garlic, minced

8 cups vegetable stock

1 (28 oz.) can diced tomatoes

⅓ cup lemon juice

½ cup agave nectar

1 head savoy cabbage

2 bay leaves

2 tsp. salt

10–15 grinds of fresh ground black pepper

½ cup fresh flat leaf parsley, plus extra for garnish

bread or salad as an accompaniment, if desired

Directions

1. Let the Home-Style Beefless Tips by Gardein sit at room temperature for about 5 minutes and cut into thin slices or shred using a fork. Set aside.

2. Sauté onions in olive oil over medium heat in large soup pot, about 5 minutes, until soft and translucent. Reduce heat, add the garlic, and continue to heat for an additional minute being careful not to burn the garlic.

3. Add beefless tips and sauté an additional five minutes, until cooked through.

4. Add remaining ingredients and simmer for 20 minutes. Discard bay leaves and add salt and pepper; the amount you add might vary based on whether or not you are using low-sodium broth.

5. Ladle into bowls and top with fresh parsley. Serve with bread and/or salad, if desired.

WHITE BEAN & FENNEL CHILI WITH MACADAMIA SOUR CREAM

Total Time: 45 minutes   Level: Easy   Serves: 6 servings

White beans and fennel are a twist on traditional chili. They give it a lighter taste that's good in winter or summer.

White Bean and Fennel Chili Ingredients

1 cup onion, diced

2 cloves garlic, minced

cooking oil, as desired

2 cans cannellini beans

½ tbsp. chili powder

1 tsp. ground cumin

1 tsp. hot sauce

1 (14.5 oz) can Muir Glen Organic Fire Roasted Diced Tomatoes

2 tsp. salt

1 tsp. oregano

2 tsp. fennel seed, crushed

fresh ground pepper, to taste

3 cups brown rice, cooked

1 red onion, chopped, for garnish

fennel fronds, for garnish

avocado, for garnish (optional)

cilantro, for garnish

Macadamia Sour Cream

Macadamia Sour Cream Ingredients

1 cup soaked macadamia nuts (soaked in water for at least 4 hours or overnight, drained)

¾ cup water

¼ cup lemon juice

½ tsp. lemon zest

½ tsp. salt

1 clove garlic

2 tbsp. grape-seed oil

(Continued)

160

White Bean and Fennel Chili Directions

1. Sauté onion and garlic in oil until translucent, about 5 minutes.

2. Add beans, chili powder, cumin, hot sauce, tomatoes, salt, oregano, and fennel seed. Cook on low heat until all flavors are blended, about 20 minutes.

3. Serve and top with red onion, fennel fronds, avocado, cilantro, and Macadamia Sour Cream (recipe below). Add additional salt and pepper to taste. Serve over 1 cup of brown rice.

Macadamia Sour Cream Directions

1. Mix all ingredients except grape-seed oil in small food processor.

2. When ingredients are fully blended, slowly pour oil in a steady stream until mixture is fully incorporated and smooth. If mixture is too try, add a little extra water.

For the Sellani's, Pasta Fagioli was a staple. Angie often used broken spaghetti (as an homage to the early days when Italians used the pasta that was available) instead of the common "ditalini" (literally, small thimbles) pasta. This was one of our father's very favorites. Try it in Week 28 (see meal plan on page 57) when using vegetable broth instead of chicken or beef broth often used in traditional pasta fagioli; you'll never miss the fat or cholesterol of those original broths.

PASTA FAGIOLI (PASTA & BEANS)

Total Time: 30 minutes   Level: Easy   Serves: 4

Ingredients

1 tbsp. olive oil

1 cup onion, chopped

½ cup celery, diced

1 cup (1 large carrot) carrot, chopped

2 cloves garlic, minced

6 cups vegetable broth

1 (28 oz.) can diced tomatoes

1 rosemary sprig

1 thyme sprig

2 bay leaves

½ cup elbow macaroni or other small pasta

1 (16 oz.) can cannellini beans, drained

juice of ½ lemon

Go Veggie! Vegan Grated Parmesan Style Topping

flat leaf Italian parsley

Directions

1. Heat olive oil in soup pot on medium heat. Add onion, celery, and carrot and sauté until softened, about five minutes.

2. Reduce heat to low and add garlic. Sauté an additional 2 minutes.

3. Add vegetable broth, tomatoes, rosemary, thyme, and bay leaves, and bring to boil.

4. When broth is boiling, add pasta. Cook until pasta is al dente (firm to the bite).

5. Add beans and stir until heated through.

6. Remove and discard rosemary, thyme, and bay leaves.

7. Squeeze fresh lemon into pot and stir. Serve immediately, topped with vegan Parmesan and fresh parsley.

INSPIRATIONAL VEGAN

TIM HAFT

Founder of Punk Rope & Beastanetics

The people in our community can have a profound impact on our lives, if we let them. Sometimes in our most vulnerable moments, we are more receptive to their influence. And often in hindsight, we gain the clarity to recall those pivotal moments when they changed the trajectory of our lives forever and for the better. For Tim Haft, one defining moment came at age fifty-one, in a New York City emergency room.

It was just after Christmas when Tim finished teaching one of his high energy Punk Rope classes in Maine. Not for the faint of heart, punk rope pushes participants to burn up to six hundred calories per hour while improving their cardio strength and endurance. A certified personal trainer and marathon coach, Tim could normally lead a class without any difficulty, but this particular frigid winter night posed a problem. He was fighting what he would later find out was a bout of pneumonia. He managed to finish teaching the class and made the long drive home to New York City where told his partner, Shana, "I think I need to go to the ER."

Doctor's Orders

Tim's ER doctor turned out to be a good friend of his, who happened to be on the night shift when he arrived. Because of their friendship, she gave him both leniency and a word of caution after examining him. She said "If I was talking to anyone else, they'd be staying in the hospital tonight. But I'm going to let you go with the provision that you take care of yourself—and you should consider going vegan." Tim recalls "She and her husband had been encouraging me for some time. It was right around the New Year and it seemed like as good a time as any to do it full on." At the time, Tim had already been a vegetarian for twenty-eight years.

Since going vegan, Tim has been in good health and has not missed a single class due to illness—and considering the intensity level of punk rope, that's saying a lot. His reasons for becoming vegetarian at the age of twenty-three were based on ethics, and as a vegan, he has gained additional health benefits and a life that is more in alignment with his values. While the ER visit spurred a prompt transition to veganism, it wasn't his first attempt to go plant-based. Tim had tried to omit dairy before without success over the past twenty-eight years. Tim thinks the difficulty was mostly psychological. "Being in New York and having access to such great pizza—that was the stumbling block for a long time. I don't know why it took me so long to get over that."

But it was more than just the pizza. He also didn't have any vegetarian, let alone vegan, friends. He didn't even have classes on animal rights or ethics, something more common in today's classrooms. And once again, community can be a powerful factor in both influence and support.

A Textbook Case for Change

His transition to vegetarianism happened in yet another unlikely place. While in a sociology class, he was reading about the industrial revolution. One of his textbooks made reference to the process of factory farming. Tim recalls, "It wasn't a critique— it was a matter-of-fact statement of how food was being produced in the twenties and thirties. I reread some of the passages and it was one of those epiphany moments where I said 'I can't do this anymore—these animals are my friends.' I gave up eating meat because of a sociology text book."

Tim's change in eating habits was based not on willpower, but on a belief system. And changes based on beliefs tend to be more sustainable. They give us an opportunity to reflect on our values, not our tastes, at every meal. After becoming vegan, Tim felt the congruence in his life and his eating habits. "I felt like for the first time I was really living my values. And that just felt right. After that, it didn't matter what anyone said. I was doing it for myself. When people ask me why, I share my story, but I don't proselytize. I try to live by example."

Problems or Opportunities?

So far, Tim turned what most people would see as restrictions into opportunities, a common trait in both vegans and entrepreneurs. The punk rope class was created after Tim had a knee injury. "I couldn't run, play basketball, soccer, or football and my world was crumbling." But he remembered back in high school that he used to jump rope to warm up before wrestling. "There is a misperception about rope jumping being hard on the knees, but it's actually very gentle. It was something I could do without pain." He also noticed that many of the fitness classes in New York were what he called "clinical and individualistic where you worked out in your own little bubble." He experimented making fitness more social. "I wanted the feeling of recess, like when we were kids, with races and games. It was an odd and interesting combination, and punk rope was born."

Punk rope classes are available around the country with a few overseas, but the element that ties them together is the idea of community. He recalls doing free demo classes to help raise money for the launch of his friend's animal shelter. "Everyone pitched in. It all incorporates the ideas of animal rights, working together, the *Peaceable Kingdom*[26]. It's something that's informed what I've done for the past eleven years. I don't force my ideals on anyone, but they know if I'm going to lead a happy hour or bar crawl there will be a ton a vegan options available."

Summary: Tim Haft

Age of Change to Veganism: 51

Current Age: 54

Statistics/Changes:

Was fit as a vegetarian, but hasn't missed a single fitness class due to illness since becoming vegan

Original Motivator/Turning Point:

An ER visit prompted by a bout of pneumonia ended with the doctor encouraging him to go vegan

Helpful Tips for New Vegans over Age 40:

"Over age 40, if you're making the transition, especially if you're living with a non-vegan partner or your family or children aren't vegan, it helps to have a community to fall back on. Books and written resources are great but it's not the same as having a couple of friends or acquaintances who can go with you to a vegan restaurant or join you once a week for a vegan potluck."

Biggest Obstacle:

Giving up New York pizza; not having friends (a community) who were vegan/vegetarian

What Helped Ease the Transition:

"Vegan desserts were good, but I was eating too many."

Questions to Consider:

1. Have you had an "epiphany" moment that revealed a conflict in your values and your behavior? Have you ever felt a conflict between your values and your food choices?

2. Do you have a community of like-minded people that would support your choice to be vegan?

3. How can you use the concept of seeing "opportunity" instead of loss when it comes to vegan eating? (e.g., joining vegan social groups, finding resources online)

4. Is there a particular food stopping you from going vegan (pizza, ice cream)? What

---

[26] *Peaceable Kingdom* is a documentary (Tribe of Heart Productions, 2004) about farmers who refuse to kill animals and convert to a vegan way of life.

viable foods substitutes are available to ease the transition?

5. What playful activities, like punk rope, do you participate in that allow you to "be a kid" again, whether through social interaction or simply by losing yourself in something fun? If you don't currently have any fun activities, what could you incorporate into your life to bring that element of fun or "recess" into your day?

BONUS RECIPE

TIM'S POWER SMOOTHIE

Ingredients

1 cup Harmless Harvest 100% Raw Coconut
    Water

2 heaping tbsp. peanut butter

1 large fistful of organic baby kale

1 cup organic mixed berries

dash of Pellegrino sparkling water

Directions

Blend until smooth. Makes roughly 1 (16 oz.) smoothie.

CHAPTER 11
Salads

"The greatness of a nation and its moral progress can be judged by the way its animals are treated."
—Gandhi

15 SHADES OF GREEN SALAD

Total Time: 20 minutes   Level: Easy   Serves: 1–2

A local Newport Beach restaurant serves incredible salads with at least fifteen different ingredients. It's like a treasure hunt in every bite, wondering what ingredient you'll discover next. I have a few variations of this salad and there's really no right or wrong way to make it. The most important thing is to get a variety of tastes, textures, and essential greens.

Ingredients

1 shaved fennel bulb

5 sugar snap peas

½ avocado, sliced

½ cup cucumber, sliced

¼ cup romaine lettuce, torn

4 Brussels sprouts, sliced thin

½ cup frisee or other salad greens

large pinch of sunflower sprouts

large pinch of pea sprouts

2 Napa cabbage leaves, torn

½ green onion, sliced diagonally

2–3 fresh mint leaves, torn

2 asparagus spears, halved lengthwise

2–3 fresh basil leaves, torn

fennel fronds for garnish

2–3 tbsp. balsamic vinegar

Directions

1. Mix all salad ingredients. Top with balsamic vinegar and serve.

Tip: Add a splash of color, if desired, with watermelon radishes, radicchio, purple carrots, and tomatoes.

CHESTNUT & ARUGULA SALAD WITH CITRUS VINAIGRETTE

Total Time: 15–25 minutes   Level: Easy   Serves: 2

Our dad loved roasted chestnuts. Whenever we make them, the aroma that fills the air can take us back decades in just an instant. This chapter will be your favorite in Week 47 (see meal plan on page 57) when we ask you to find plant-based salad dressings.

Chestnut & Arugula Salad Ingredients

1 cup chestnuts, raw, or precooked and packaged

2 cups arugula

1 head radicchio or red lettuce

½ red onion, sliced thin

1 apple, diced, plus extra for garnish

1 celery stalk, sliced

2 tbsp. dried cranberries

Citrus Vinaigrette

Citrus Vinaigrette Ingredients

½ cup orange juice

½ tbsp. olive oil

2 tbsp. apple cider vinegar

1 pinch salt

¼ tsp. minced garlic

zest of 1 orange

orange wedges

Chestnut & Arugula Salad Directions

1. If using raw chestnuts, rinse thoroughly. Then score each one by making two slits in the shape of a long "x" on the round side. Place on a baking pan underneath the broiler for 5–10 minutes until they open up at the cut seam. Turn periodically for even cooking.

(Continued)

2. Remove when shells start to scorch and the chestnut meat is golden brown—keep an eye on them so they don't burn. Wrap the chestnuts in a dishcloth to cool; this will allow them to steam and open. Then peel and cut in halves or quarters for the salad. If using precooked chestnuts, remove from the package and cut in halves or quarters.

3. Mix chestnuts with all salad ingredients and toss with Citrus Vinaigrette (recipe below).

Citrus Vinaigrette Directions

1. Blend all ingredients in blender until mixed.

> **Tip:** Try Blanchard and Blanchard vinaigrette in the foil package, usually found near the produce section of the supermarket.

ASIAN CUCUMBER SALAD

Total Time: 5 minutes   Level: Easy   Serves: 2

Ingredients:

2 small Persian cucumbers or ½ hot house cucumber

1 tsp. Eden Foods Hot Pepper Sesame Oil

1 tbsp. rice wine vinegar

¼ tsp. fresh ginger, peeled and grated

1 tsp. agave

1 tsp. sesame seeds, black or white

Directions:

1. Slice cucumbers in paper thin slices using a mandoline or knife—use extreme caution when using a mandoline.

2. Mix sesame oil, rice wine vinegar, ginger, and agave thoroughly.

3. Pour over cucumbers and top with sesame seeds.

CHOPPED FENNEL SALAD WITH TART CHERRY VINAIGRETTE

Total Time: 20 minutes   Level: Easy   Serves: 2

Chopped Fennel Salad Ingredients

3 cups raw vegetables of your choice, finely chopped (Ex: fennel (bulb), carrots, red cabbage, savoy cabbage, radish, broccoli)

½ avocado, sliced thin, for garnish

2 tbsp. dried tart cherries or dried cranberries, for garnish

2 tbsp. slivered almonds, for garnish

Tart Cherry Vinaigrette Ingredients

6 tbsp. Dynamic Health Tart Cherry Juice Concentrate

3 tbsp. rice wine vinegar

1 tbsp. agave nectar

1½ tsp. fennel seeds, crushed

2 tbsp. chives, finely chopped, for garnish (optional)

Chopped Fennel Salad Directions

1. Portion the chopped vegetables on two plates.

2. Garnish each salad with avocado, cherries or cranberries, and almonds.

4. Garnish with chives, if desired.

Tart Cherry Vinaigrette Directions

1. Mix all vinaigrette ingredients with wire whisk and serve with salad.

Tip: Tart cherry juice promotes healthy sleep, so you might want to have this salad for dinner rather than lunch.

Tip: A Ninja personal blender is ideal for this dressing because it's such a small amount.

SUSAN'S FAVORITE CHOPPED SALAD

Total Time: 20 minutes   Level: Easy   Serves: 2

When Susan comes to visit me in California, we head to her favorite restaurant for chopped salad. The lemony garlic dressing makes it a perfect summer entrée.

Susan's Favorite Chopped Salad Ingredients

1 heart of Romaine lettuce, chopped

½ cup cherry tomatoes

½ avocado, diced

1 ear of fresh or cooked corn

1 apple, cored and diced

½ cup cashews, chopped

½ cup fresh flat leaf parsley, chopped, loosely packed

Lemon Vinaigrette Dressing Ingredients

4 tbsp. fresh squeezed lemon juice

½ tbsp. EVOO

1 small garlic clove

6 large fresh basil leaves

generous pinch of salt

several grinds of fresh black pepper, to taste

Susan's Favorite Chopped Salad Directions

1. Toss all ingredients in a bowl with Lemon Vinaigrette Dressing (recipe to follow).

2. Serve with additional avocado slices and fresh cracked black pepper.

Lemon Vinaigrette Dressing Directions

1. Mix all ingredients together in a small blender until thoroughly incorporated.

CITRUS QUINOA SALAD WITH TOASTED HAZELNUTS

Total Time: 20 minutes   Level: Easy   Serves: 2–3 entrée-sized salads

Crunchy hazelnuts, colorful veggies, and a citrusy dressing make this salad both light and satisfying.

Salad Ingredients

½ cup tricolored quinoa

½ cup water

1 cup Persian cucumber, chopped

1 celery stalk, chopped

1 cup red, yellow, or green pepper, chopped

½ cup carrots, chopped

2 green onions, thinly sliced

1 tbsp. fresh mint, minced

3 tbsp. chopped hazelnuts, toasted in a shallow pan on low heat until brown

1 cup grape tomatoes

2 tsp. fresh basil, cut into thin ribbons

salt and fresh ground black pepper, to taste

Dressing

2 tbsp. balsamic vinegar

1 tbsp. agave nectar

1 tbsp. lemon juice

½ tsp. red pepper flakes

¼ tsp. sea salt

1 clove garlic

Salad Directions

1. Combine quinoa and water. Bring to a boil. Cover, reduce heat to low, and simmer until tender, about 15 minutes. Drain thoroughly.

2. Toss cucumber, celery, pepper, carrots, onions, and mint in a mixing bowl. Spoon quinoa into dishes or use a ring mold to give it form and height.

(Continued)

3. Serve with Dressing (recipe below) and top with toasted hazelnuts, grape tomatoes, fresh ground fresh basil, salt, and pepper.

Dressing Directions

1. Combine all dressing ingredients in high speed blender until fully incorporated.

TABBOULEH-STYLE BEAN SALAD

Total Time: 20 minutes   Level: Easy   Serves: 2

Tabbouleh is a Middle Eastern dish usually made with bulgur, a type of quick-cooking wheat. The herbs and lemon make it incredibly fresh and satisfying. In this version, we've replaced the wheat with beans and used a fraction of the olive oil. The salad is loaded with flavor and has significantly less fat.

Salad Ingredients

1 can garbanzo beans (drain and reserve the liquid or "aquafaba")

1 cup fresh flat-leaf parsley leaves, minced

3 tbsp. fresh mint, finely chopped

1 small tomato, seeded and small diced

3 scallions, thinly sliced

Dressing Ingredients

¼ cup lemon juice

1 tsp. olive oil

1 garlic clove, minced

¼ tsp. salt

fresh cracked black pepper, to taste

Salad Directions

1. Place all salad ingredients in a salad bowl. Toss Dressing (recipe below) with salad and serve.

Dressing Directions

1. In blender, combine lemon juice, olive oil, garlic clove, salt, and pepper until thoroughly blended.

ASIAN PEAR, PINK GRAPEFRUIT & AVOCADO SALAD

Total Time: 20 minutes   Level: Easy   Serves: 2

This salad is so impressive because of its beautiful pink, white, and green color palette, black sesame seed garnish, and the subtle heat of the Asian-inspired dressing. Serve this when you want to impress.

Dressing Ingredients

2 tsp. rice vinegar

1 tsp. agave nectar

½ tsp. hot pepper sesame oil

fresh ginger, to taste, peeled and grated on Microplane or other fine grater

Salad Ingredients

1 avocado, pitted, sliced ¼-inch thick

1 large ruby red grapefruit, peeled, cut into sections

1 Asian pear, core removed, sliced

½ cup sunflower sprouts, for garnish

½ tbsp. black sesame seeds, for garnish

Dressing Directions

1. Mix dressing ingredients and set aside.

Salad Directions

1. Arrange the avocado, grapefruit, and pear, rotating with alternate slices.
2. Drizzle salad with dressing and garnish with sprouts and sesame seeds.

HARVEST SALAD WITH PUMPKIN VINAIGRETTE

Total Time: 20 minutes   Level: Easy   Serves: 4

Pumpkin adds creaminess to vinaigrette and gives you a dose of Vitamin A, which plays a critical role in healthy vision. The dressing recipe makes more than you'll need for the salad. Store it in the fridge for up to 3 days and use it as a dip for raw veggies.

Salad Ingredients

2 cups radicchio or romaine lettuce, torn

2 cups curly endive, torn

4 baby red potatoes, steamed and quartered

8 asparagus spears, steamed

1 celery stalk, diced

1 head cauliflower florets

4 pecans, halved

4 dates, pitted and small diced

1 red Bartlett pear, cut into thin slices

4 tbsp. pumpkin seeds, shelled

microgreens, for garnish (optional)

Dressing Ingredients

1 cup canned pumpkin

¼ cup olive oil plus 2 tbsp.

1 garlic clove

5 tbsp. balsamic vinegar

1 tbsp. agave nectar

⅛ tsp. pumpkin pie spice

4–5 grinds of fresh black peppercorns

¼ tsp. salt, to taste

Salad Directions

1. Drizzle 1-2 tbsp. of dressing on each plate using a spoon or squeeze bottle.

2. Arrange the radicchio leaves and longer pieces of endives on the plate.

(Continued)

3. Mix the remaining ingredients except pumpkin seeds in a separate bowl without dressing, to fully incorporate.

4. Add the ingredients to the plate and garnish with pumpkin seeds and/or microgreens.

Dressing Directions

1. Combine all ingredients except oil in blender. When fully blended, drizzle olive oil in slowly until fully incorporated.

2. Serving size is 1 to 2 tbsp. per person. Save the rest in the fridge for up to one week.

PANZANELLA
(ITALIAN BREAD SALAD)

Total Time: 90 minutes   Level: Easy   Serves: 2

Our grandmothers would laugh if they knew we were sharing the recipe for Panzanella, considered to be a "poor man's dish." This is what Italians did with leftover stale bread; they were masters of the "reduce, reuse, recycle" habit long before it became cool. If you don't have stale bread, you can toast your bread in the oven to enjoy Panzanella.

Salad Ingredients

4 heirloom tomatoes, chopped into 1-inch squares or grape heirloom tomatoes, sliced lengthwise

½ (4 cups) loaf of stale crusty, hearty Italian or sourdough bread cut into 1-inch cubes. (If the bread is not stale, heat in the oven at 300°F until dry but not toasted, about 15 minutes.)

½ red onion, thinly sliced

1 (½-inch) English cucumber, sliced and halved

1 cup fresh basil, cut into ribbons

Dressing Ingredients

½ cup balsamic vinegar

2–3 garlic cloves, crushed

3 tbsp. olive oil

salt & pepper, to taste

Salad Directions

1. Fill mixing bowl with tomatoes, bread, onion, and cucumber.

2. Add dressing (recipe below) and toss thoroughly, making sure bread cubes are coated.

3. Let sit for one hour, mixing occasionally to ensure the dressing is being absorbed evenly throughout.

4. Top with fresh basil, stir thoroughly, and serve.

(Continued)

Dressing Directions

1. Combine vinegar, garlic, and oil in a food processor or whisk by hand until thoroughly incorporated. Add salt and pepper to taste.

KALE SALAD
WITH ORANGE VINAIGRETTE

Total Time: 15   Level: Easy   Serves: 2

Kale Salad Ingredients

2 cups kale leaves, chopped, center stems
   removed

1 cup Brussels Sprouts, sliced thin

½ cucumber, sliced

3 tbsp. Marcona almonds

½ avocado, diced small

½ orange, rind removed, cut into small
   sections

2 tbsp. green onion, sliced at an angle

2 tbsp. flat leaf parsley, chopped

½ cup dried cranberries

Orange Vinaigrette Ingredients

6 tbsp. orange juice

2 tbsp. rice wine vinegar

1 tbsp. agave nectar

1 garlic clove, minced

salt & fresh ground black pepper, to taste

Kale Salad Directions

1. Toss all salad ingredients in a large serving bowl.

2. Serve with Orange Vinaigrette (recipe directions below).

Orange Vinaigrette Directions

1. Combine ingredients with wire whisk or put in small blender or food processor and mix until
    thoroughly combined.

ROASTED CAULIFLOWER SALAD

This was always a popular vegetable in our house. We served the traditional white cauliflower steamed with a little salt and pepper. This version adds extra flavor and crunch. The colored cauliflower varieties make this dish beautiful enough to be a main course. It holds up well in the fridge for a few days so it's ideal for Week 29 (see meal plan on page 57) when you'll be focusing on placing irresistible salads front and center in your fridge.

Ingredients

7 cups purple, green, or yellow cauliflower

3 tbsp. EVOO

5 whole cloves garlic

½ tbsp. salt

fresh ground black pepper, to taste

½ tsp. red pepper flakes

½ cup panko breadcrumbs

¼ cup fresh squeezed lemon juice

1 cup. flat leaf parsley leaves, loosely packed

1 red apple, small diced

Directions

1. Preheat oven to 450°F.
2. In large baking pan with raised edges mix the cauliflower, olive oil, garlic, salt, pepper, and red pepper flakes until thoroughly combined.
3. Roast the cauliflower mixture for 25 minutes, stirring occasionally.
4. After 25 minutes, stir in the breadcrumbs thoroughly and continue to roast for another 10 minutes.
5. Remove from oven and place in bowl. Add lemon juice, parsley, and apple and stir thoroughly.
6. Serve warm as a main course or a side salad.

INSPIRATIONAL VEGAN

SHARON PALMER

RDN, Author, Journalist

When was the last time your doctor looked at your medical record and said "I feel like I'm looking at the chart of a teenager"? That's what Sharon Palmer's physician told her five years ago, when she had just turned fifty years old. At the time, Sharon had been eating a plant-based diet for about a year. But it's what her doctor said next that prompted an immediate response from Sharon. He added, "You have good genes."

Sharon quickly corrected him. "No, I have a family history of cancer, heart disease, and obesity." Sharon knew despite her family history, she could take control of her health by switching to a vegan diet, and she knew just how to make the switch. Sharon is a registered dietitian. Her smart approach to eating vegan demonstrates that, regardless of your age or genetic blueprint, you can make dramatic improvements to your health with a whole food, plant-based diet. As Sharon says emphatically, "It's never too late to go vegan."

With 850 articles to her credit in publications like *Better Homes & Gardens, Prevention, Oxygen, LA Times,* and *Cooking Smart,* Sharon is an undeniable expert on plant-based living. The author of two books, *The Plant-Powered Diet* and *Plant-Powered for Life*[27], editor of the acclaimed health newsletter, *Environmental Nutrition,* and

---

[27]http://sharonpalmer.com/book.php

nutrition editor for *Today's Dietitian*, Sharon's nutritional roots run deep. Her award-winning *Plant-Powered Blog*[28] features daily tips, interviews, and recipes to take the guess work out of vegan living. Even her degree was earned from a school that is known for its plant-centric ideology. In 2013, Sharon was honored with a Distinguished Alumnus Award from Southern California's Loma Linda University. The city of Loma Linda is identified as a one of the world's five "Blue Zones," geographic pockets where people reach age one hundred at a rate ten times greater than anywhere else in the US. One of the nine characteristics common to Blue Zones is a plant-based diet.[29]

Contrast Sharon's comprehensive knowledge base with that of the average doctor who has roughly between six and fourteen hours of nutrition education as part of their medical school curriculum.[30] This disparity in training underscores the importance of consulting with a dietitian when making any changes to your diet, especially in the second half of life.

Sharon's 30-Day Challenge

Sharon's medical statistics were always in the healthy range, having spent most of

her life as a vegetarian. But her numbers went from good to great after she made the switch to veganism and eliminated all animal products from her diet.

"To do research for my book in 2010, I put myself on a vegan challenge for thirty days. At the time, I was lacto-ovo (eating dairy and eggs but no meat, chicken, or fish). After the vegan challenge I thought, 'This is not that hard.'" Her experiment paid off. "My CRP (a blood test that measures inflammation in the body), cholesterol, glucose, and blood pressure all improved. I felt so good about the impact on my health and the planet, I've stayed vegan ever since."

Her doctor wasn't the only one who noticed the change. Sharon adds, "People told me my skin looked better. Most people think I'm ten years younger than I am. It could be because of the high level of antioxidants and the low level of inflammatory components in a vegan diet."

[28]http://sharonpalmer.com/blog.php
[29]https://www.bluezones.com/2014/03/blue-zones-history/
[30]http://www.hindawi.com/journals/jbe/2015/357627/tab1/

And while Sharon was at a healthy weight range, she did end up several pounds lighter, often a by-product of the vegan diet. She adds, "Studies consistently show that vegans on average weigh significantly less than their omnivorous counterparts."

A Dietician's Approach to Going Vegan

Sharon, who speaks regularly on diet and nutrition, is often asked if age is a factor in becoming vegan. "I get asked by older women, even those in their sixties and seventies, 'Am I too old to become vegan?' and I say 'No, if you have a well-balanced diet, you can be vegan at any time of your life.'"

Sharon stresses the importance of making a smart transition, especially if you are over the age of forty. "Most people wing it. They just avoid animal products, but it's not about eating vegan brownies and French fries. When you get older, your nutritional intake is even more important. Older people need more protein then we previously thought." Sharon recommends every meal and snack contain a quality source of plant protein: tofu, legumes, nuts, or seeds. Sharon also recommends eating leafy green and cruciferous vegetables daily for plant calcium.

Don't Forget Your Supplements

Sharon emphasizes the importance of supplements, especially in the second half of life. "The Institute of Medicine says that everyone over the age of fifty should take B12—it's not just a vegan problem. Up to 30 percent of people over fifty may not adequately absorb B12 from food sources due to a decrease in digestive enzymes or stomach acid and should consider eating foods fortified with B12 or using a B12 supplement.[31] And vegans—no matter what their age—should ensure they are meeting their B12 needs through supplements or fortified foods."

Sharon also takes a multivitamin every other day. "Studies show that vegans get a lot more than the RDA of lots of vitamins and minerals, but iodine may be a concern. A multivitamin is an insurance policy for me. On top of that, I take 500 mg of calcium on top of my dietary intake of calcium as a precaution to keep my bones strong. Research shows that vegans' risk of osteoporosis is the same as the general population if they meet their calcium, protein, and vitamin D needs." She also takes Vitamin D daily, along with outdoor

---

[31] Food and Nutrition Board, Institute of Medicine. "Dietary Reference Intakes for Thiamin, Riboflavin, Niacin, Vitamin B6, Folate, Vitamin B12, Pantothenic Acid, Biotin, and Choline." Washington, DC: National Academy Press; 2000

activities several times a week, and a marine algae omega-3 supplement three times a week. It's important to note that everyone's needs are different, and your supplement program should be discussed with your dietician or physician.

Moving Along the Plant-Based Food Spectrum

Sharon speaks of a plant-based lifestyle in terms of a continuum, with veganism being the most plant-based diet and flexitarian being the least. While she believes the vegan end of the spectrum is the healthiest, she also acknowledges that some people are more successful with a step-by-step approach, adding more plants to their existing diets. The USDA agrees, advocating that a diet rich in fruit and vegetables can reduce the risk for heart disease, obesity, and Type 2 diabetes, protect against certain types of cancers, lower blood pressure, reduce the development of kidney stones, and decrease bone loss.[32]

Where Do I Begin?

If you've been a lifelong omnivore, or even a vegetarian, you might wonder how to become vegan in a healthy way. It could be as simple as following Sharon's lead and giving yourself a challenge within a specific time frame. Sharon gave herself thirty days, but if you want to take a smaller step, consider a two-week plan.

The 14 Day Plant-Powered Menu Planner from Sharon's book, *The Plant Powered Diet* (The Experiment, 2014), helps people get started with a tasty range of nutrient-rich foods and recipes. Tested in her own kitchen, these meals are enough to convince anyone about the perks of eating plants. Imagine a menu that includes pumpkin pecan spice pancakes, a grilled vegetable and pesto panini, and country berry cobbler. You'll soon learn that Sharon's plan isn't going to look like the celery stalk and rice cake starvation diets you've experienced in the past. And when you are able to eat delicious foods that make you feel healthy and vibrant, you might just want to continue long after the two-week challenge ends. At the very least, you will know what a balanced menu looks like and you'll have more vegan recipes to add to your repertoire. And, if you stick with it, there's a good chance you'll have one other enviable benefit— hearing your own doctor say that you have the medical chart of a teenager.

---

[32]http://www.choosemyplate.gov/vegetables-nutrients-health

Summary: Sharon Palmer
Age of Change to Veganism: 49
Current Age: 54

Statistics/Changes:

- Improvements in blood CRP (a blood test that measures inflammation in the body), cholesterol, glucose, and blood pressure
- Better skin, younger-looking appearance
- Better resistance to fighting colds

Original Motivator & Turning Point:

- Family with a history of cancer, heart disease, and obesity
- Long-standing experience with vegetarian living and knowledge as a dietitian
- Gave herself a 30-day vegan challenge while writing her book on plant-based living

Helpful Tips for New Vegans Over Age 40:

- Consult with a dietitian experienced in this diet
- Take the right supplements and eat a balanced whole food diet

Practical Tips:

- Social situations are a challenge. Prepare yourself for how you will eat out in a restaurant, and dine with people who aren't vegan. Being vegan is easy in your own home, but you must develop a sense of how you will navigate it in social settings.

What Helped Ease the Transition:

- My favorite thing to do at a restaurant is to tell the waiter right off the bat that I'm vegan and see if the chef wants to make me something. Sometimes that turns out to be the best food. Chefs in some of the better restaurants usually love the challenge.

Questions to Consider:

- How do I feel about my last doctor's visit and set of medical tests: heart rate, blood pressure, cholesterol, weight, etc.?
- When was the last time I discussed nutrition with my physician? A dietician?
- Would I be more successful going "cold turkey" to a vegan diet or a step-by-step approach?
- How can I prepare to deal with social situations when eating vegan? (e.g., bringing a vegan entrée to a potluck to ensure I had something to eat.)
- How comfortable do I feel asking for a vegan entrée at a restaurant? How supportive would my friends be of my change in dietary habits?

BONUS RECIPE

SHARON'S TORTILLA SOUP

Tortilla Strip Ingredients

3 (6-inch) corn tortillas

2 tsp. EVOO

½ tsp. chili powder

Soup Ingredients

2 tsp. EVOO

1 medium onion, diced

1 medium garlic clove, minced

1 medium green bell pepper, diced

1 small jalapeño pepper, finely diced

1 small zucchini, diced

1 cup frozen corn

¼ tsp. crushed red pepper

2 tsp. cumin

4 cups water

1 tbsp. reduced sodium vegetable broth base

2 (14.5 oz.) cans diced tomatoes, with liquid

1 (15 oz.) can black beans, with liquid (or 1¾ cups cooked, with ½ cup water)

⅔ cup plant-based cheese, optional

⅔ cup green onions, chopped

Tortilla Strip Directions

1. Preheat the oven to 400°F

2. Slice the tortillas into thin strips. Place them on a baking sheet and drizzle with 2 teaspoons of olive oil, then sprinkle the chili powder on top. Bake for about 5 to 8 minutes, until brown and crisp. Remove from oven and set aside. Turn off the oven.

(Continued)

Soup Directions

1. Heat the 2 teaspoons of olive oil in a large pot over medium heat. Add the onion and sauté for 5 minutes.

2. Add the garlic, bell pepper, jalapeño, zucchini, corn, crushed red pepper, and cumin and sauté for an additional 5 minutes.

3. Add the water, broth base, tomatoes, and black beans. Stir well and cover. Simmer over medium heat for 25 to 30 minutes, until vegetables are tender.

4. Ladle about 1 cup of soup into soup bowls, and garnish with a few tortilla strips, 1 tablespoon of plant-based cheese, and 1 tablespoon green onions. Serve immediately.

5. Store leftover soup (without garnishes) in the refrigerator for up to three days. Reheat the soup and garnish with the tortilla strips, cheese, and green onions.

Per Serving: 148 calories, 5 g protein, 21 g carbohydrate, 5 g fat, 1 g saturated fat, 5 g fiber, 5 g sugar, 263 mg sodium

Star Nutrients: vitamin C (40% DV), folate (12% DV), calcium (14% DV), manganese (11% DV), molybdenum (44% DV), phosphorus (10% DV), potassium (10% DV)

CHAPTER 12

Entrées

"Animals are here with us, not for us."
—Anonymous

BROCCOLI & PASTA

Total Time: 30 minutes   Level: Easy   Serves: 6

This simple dish always gets rave reviews. Cook the broccoli just enough to get it tender while still bright green in color. Sprinkle generously with Go Veggie! Parmesan Style topping, a must-have in Week 32 (see meal plan on page 57), when you'll discover so many wonderful cheese substitutes. This one is very authentic in flavor and texture.

Ingredients

3 quarts (12 cups) water

½ tbsp. salt

1 lb. box of pasta (e.g., elbow macaroni, small shells)

2 large heads of broccoli

1 tbsp. olive oil

2 large cloves of garlic, minced

salt & pepper, to taste

pinch red pepper flakes

Go Veggie! Vegan Grated Parmesan Style Topping

Directions

1. Bring water to boil in pot. Add salt to water and boil macaroni or shells until firm to the bite. Drain the pasta and reserve 1 cup of pasta water.

2. Remove thick stems from broccoli and discard or save for stock. Cut florets into bite-sized pieces. Rinse thoroughly.

3. Steam broccoli in steamer over boiling water until tender but firm, about 5 minutes. It should be a bright green color—do not overcook.

4. Remove broccoli from steamer and sauté in non-stick frying pan on low to medium heat with olive oil and garlic for 3 minutes, stirring occasionally so garlic does not burn and flavors become fully incorporated. Add salt and pepper to taste. If mixture gets too dry, use some of the reserved pasta water.

5. Add the pasta to the pan and thoroughly mix the pasta with the broccoli mixture. Add a pinch of red pepper flakes, if desired.

6. Ladle onto plates and top with vegan Parmesan cheese.

MANICOTTI FLORENTINE WITH CASHEW RICOTTA

Total Time: 50 minutes   Level: Medium   Serves: 7 (2 shells per person)

Man-i-KOT-ee. Even the name sounds magical. These "cheesy "stuffed cylinders are filled with cashew ricotta and spinach and topped with zesty marinara. Try our homemade marinara sauce recipe (page 216) as recommended in Week 30 (see meal plan on page 57).

Cashew Ricotta Ingredients

3½ cups raw cashews soaked for at least 4 hours or overnight

1 cup water

½ cup lemon juice

1 tsp. lemon zest

1 tsp. minced garlic

1 large pinch onion powder

1 cup nutritional yeast

1½ tsp. salt

4 tbsp. flax meal

2 tbsp. Go Veggie! Vegan Grated Parmesan Style Topping, plus extra for garnish

2 (10 oz.) package of frozen chopped spinach, thawed and drained with water squeezed out

Manicotti Florentine Ingredients

1 (8 oz.) box of manicotti shells

1 (24–26 oz.) jar of good quality vegan marinara sauce

fresh basil or flat leaf parsley, for garnish

Cashew Ricotta Directions

1. Mix all ingredients except the flax meal, Parmesan, and spinach in a high-powered blender like a Vitamix until creamy. You might have to add a little more water if the mixture feels too dry and stop occasionally to scrape the sides while blending. It should be about the consistency of a thick muffin batter. *(Continued)*

2. Put the cheese mixture into a bowl and fold in flax meal, Parmesan, and spinach until fully incorporated. Set aside. The mixture will thicken up a bit as it sits.

Manicotti Florentine Directions

1. Preheat oven to 400°F.

2. Boil manicotti shells according to package directions.

3. Remove manicotti shells carefully and set on flat surface until cool enough to handle.

4. Put the Cashew Ricotta mixture (recipe above) into a pastry bag or a plastic bag with the tip cut off. Hold the shells and fill with the mixture.

5. Spread a light coating of sauce into the bottom of a 13 x 9-inch baking dish to prevent pasta from sticking.

6. Place the shells side by side in the baking dish and pour the remaining sauce over the top.

7. Cover the pan with foil and cook for 30 minutes.

8. Remove from oven and let cook for about 10 minutes. Sprinkle with vegan Parmesan and fresh basil or flat leaf parsley.

Tip: Classico or Barilla brands are great in Tomato Basil. If you have a little extra time, you can also make our homemade Easy Marinara recipe (page 216).

NUT LOAF

Total Time: 2 hours   Level: Easy   Serves: 8

This is a classic "meatloaf" recipe using beans and walnuts to give a hearty texture. The ketchup topping will take you back to your childhood. Serve with mashed potatoes for a taste of healthy nostalgia. Leftovers make great sandwich fillings, especially during Week 25 (see meal plan on page 57), when you'll be looking for a meaty substitute for traditional hamburgers.

Nut Loaf Ingredients

1 can cannellini beans, reserve liquid (aquafaba) and set aside. Rinse beans thoroughly with water

1 cup walnuts, soaked for at least 1 hour or overnight, drained

½ cup onion, finely diced

2 celery stalks, finely diced

6 tbsp. aquafaba (liquid from the can of beans)

1½ cups panko breadcrumbs

½ cup almond milk

1 tsp. salt

several grinds of black pepper, to taste

red pepper flakes (optional)

Sauce Ingredients

½ cup Annie's Naturals Organic Ketchup

2 tbsp. organic brown sugar

1 tbsp. yellow prepared mustard

large pinch of red pepper flakes

Nut Loaf Directions

1. Preheat oven to 350°F.

2. Pulse beans and walnuts in a food processor until combined, but do not overmix. Mixture should resemble ground turkey and have some texture to it.

(Continued)

Bowness Library
Self Checkout

July,09,2019 18:54

39065152034714   2019-07-30
The 40-year-old vegan : 75 recipes to m
ake you leaner, cleaner, and greener in
the second half of life

Total   1 item(s)

You have 0 item(s) ready for pickup

3. Mix onion, celery, aquafaba, panko breadcrumbs, almond milk, salt, and pepper in a bowl until thoroughly combined. It's easiest if you use your hands.

4. Press mixture firmly into 8 x 4-inch loaf pan.

5. Stir sauce ingredients (recipe below) and pour on top of nut loaf.

6. Bake for 1½ hours uncovered. Let sit for 5 minutes after removing from oven. Slice and serve with mashed potatoes or your favorite side dish.

Sauce Directions

1. Combine all ingredients and serve over nut loaf.

This creamy pesto sauce is filled with fresh flavor and makes a perfect topping for these easy zucchini noodles. Try this during Week 32 (see meal plan on page 57) when you're craving something cheesy like traditional pesto.

ZUCCHINI PASTA WITH LEMON WALNUT PESTO

Total Time: 20 minutes   Level: Easy   Serves 4

Lemon Walnut Pesto Ingredients

2 cups zucchini, cubed

½ cup walnuts, plus extra for garnish

½ cup avocado

1 clove garlic, sliced

1 cup fresh basil leaves, tightly packed, plus extra for garnish

⅓ cup fresh squeezed lemon juice

½ tsp. salt

¼ tsp. red pepper flakes, plus extra for garnish

fresh ground black pepper, to taste

Zucchini Pasta Ingredients

4 whole zucchini

Lemon Walnut Pesto Directions

1. In blender, mix cubed zucchini until liquefied. Add remaining ingredients and blend until combined into a creamy sauce. Set aside.

Zucchini Pasta Directions

1. Take whole zucchini and cut the small ends off each one. Run each zucchini through a spiralizer to create noodles. The noodles will be long, so you can cut them into spaghetti-length pieces to make eating easier. If you do not have a spiralizer, you can use a potato peeler to make long zucchini "strips."

2. Top zucchini noodles with lemon walnut pesto and garnish with additional chopped walnuts, fresh basil leaves, and red pepper flakes.

ASIAN STYLE DUMPLINGS

Total Time: 35 minutes   Level: Medium   Serves: 5–6

It's not surprising we love dumplings—they're a twist on ravioli. These are so simple to make and will taste like you've been working on them all day. In Week 51 (see meal plan on page 57), we recommend a vegan version of Asian fried rice.

Ingredients

1 tsp. oil

¼ tsp. sesame chili oil, plus extra for garnish

1 cup leek (white part only), thoroughly cleaned and minced

2 garlic cloves, minced

3 cups Napa cabbage, shredded

½ cup carrot shredded with hand grater or minced

1 cup baby spinach, cut into thin strips

2 tsp. fresh ginger, grated with Microplane or other fine grater, or thoroughly minced

1 tbsp. soy sauce, plus extra for garnish

1 tsp. agave nectar

¼ cup fresh cilantro

1 (28–30) package commercially prepared won ton wrappers (read ingredients to make sure they do not contain dairy)

2–4 cups water or more depending on the size of your pot

sesame seeds, black, white or both, for garnish

green onions, cut diagonally

Directions

1. In a large pan sauté leek and garlic in oil and sesame chili oil on medium low heat until softened, about 3 minutes.

2. Add cabbage, carrot, spinach, ginger, soy sauce, and agave and continue to mix until all vegetables are softened, about another 3 minutes.

3. Transfer mixture to bowl with slotted spoon, to omit extra liquid. Add fresh cilantro and mix thoroughly.

(Continued)

212

4. Place won ton wrappers on a cutting board. Scoop a teaspoon of the vegetable mixture into the center of the won ton wrapper. Dip your fingers into water and wet all four edges of the wrapper.

5. Place a steamer basket into a pot that contains 2 to 4 cups water while preparing dumplings. The amount of water will vary depending on the size of your pot and the height of your steamer basket. The water level should be below the steamer basket, allowing it to steam the dumplings without touching them. Bring the water to a boil.

6. Pull all corners of the won ton inward until they touch. Pinch the sides together to form four "seams." While doing this, push any air out of the dumpling to form a tight little package.

7. Place dumplings into the steamer basket. Leave a little space on the sides of each dumpling so they don't stick together. In an average size steamer basket, you should be able to fit about 6 dumplings.

8. Let the dumplings steam for 2 minutes. Carefully remove dumplings and repeat until all dumplings are cooked.

9. Place the dumplings on a dish and drizzle with just a touch of soy sauce, sesame chili oil, white and black sesame seeds, and sliced green onion.

GROWN-UP MAC & CHEESE CASSEROLE

Total Time: 30 minutes   Level: Easy   Serves: 2 as a main dish; 4 as a side dish

We never outgrow the ultimate comfort food—mac and cheese. As little girls, we used to eat an entire box together. As adults, we all want something with ingredients we can feel good about. This recipe uses nutritional yeast and lemon for a tangy, cheesy flavor. The breadcrumbs add some crunch and parsley gives a fresh flavor that you'll never get from a box. You can also add in steamed broccoli for extra color, nutrients, and texture. You'll especially appreciate this in Week 32 (see meal plan on page 57), when you'll discover there are so many cholesterol free cheese substitutes. This will become a new classic recipe.

Ingredients

1½ tbsp. olive oil

1½ tbsp. unbleached, all-purpose flour

2 tbsp. nutritional yeast

½ cup cashew milk or other nut milk

⅛ tsp. onion salt

⅛ tsp. garlic salt

½ tsp. sweet paprika

1 tsp. agave nectar

¾ tsp. salt

3 tbsp. lemon juice

pinch red pepper flakes, plus extra for garnish

1 cup elbow macaroni

4 tbsp. panko breadcrumbs (these will add the crunchy top to your casserole)

salt and fresh ground black pepper, to taste

olive oil spray

fresh flat leaf parsley

Directions

1. Make a roux by heating olive oil in a saucepan with the flour on low heat. Mix thoroughly until thick and bubbly, about 1 minute, stirring constantly.

2. Add nutritional yeast, milk, onion salt, garlic salt, paprika, agave, salt, lemon juice, and red pepper flakes. Stir until fully blended.

(Continued)

214

3. Cook pasta according to package directions. Drain pasta and toss with cheese sauce.

4. Separate pasta into a small broiler-safe baking dish.

5. Sprinkle with breadcrumbs, a pinch of salt, and spray with olive oil. Heat under broiler until breadcrumbs start to brown, 3 to 5 minutes.

6. Remove from broiler and add additional salt, pepper, red pepper flakes, and paprika to taste.

7. Garnish with fresh flat leaf parsley to add a fresh taste to this rich, hearty dish.

Tip: You can add your favorite vegetable to this dish, such as steamed broccoli, peas, or carrots. You can also serve as is with a fresh garden salad.

EASY PASTA
WITH MARINARA SAUCE

Total Time: 25 minutes   Level: Easy   Serves: 4–6

This is a classic recipe you can whip up in minutes. You'll be tempted just to eat it directly from the pan using a piece of crusty Italian bread as your spoon. Week 23 (see meal plan on page 57) recommends bringing a great homemade marinara sauce when dining at a friend's house.

Ingredients

2 tbsp. olive oil

2 tbsp. fresh garlic cloves, minced

1 (28 oz). can Muir Glen Organic Diced Tomatoes

1 tsp. salt

1 tbsp. dried basil

1–2 pinches red pepper flakes, to taste

5 grinds of fresh black pepper

1 pound of vegan, regular, or gluten free pasta (we like Barilla)

fresh basil leaves, cut into ribbons

Go Veggie! Vegan Grated Parmesan Style Topping, for garnish

Directions

1. Heat olive oil and garlic on low to medium heat in a nonstick skillet. Sauté about 5 minutes until the garlic starts to become aromatic. Garlic should get warm but be careful not to burn it or it will become bitter.

2. Add diced tomatoes to pan and bring to boil.

3. Add salt, basil, and red pepper flakes and reduce heat to a low simmer.

4. Let sauce simmer uncovered for 10 minutes, stirring occasionally. The sauce should be bubbling slightly but not boiling.

5. If the sauce it too chunky for your taste, you can either break up the tomatoes with a wooden spoon or use an immersion blender and blend until you achieve the texture you

(Continued)

216

desire. If you want a completely smooth sauce, you can use canned tomato sauce instead of diced tomatoes or you can put all of the sauce in a blender and purée until completely smooth. Add fresh ground black pepper.

6. The sauce will be just a bit salty but remember, you're going to be putting it on top of plain pasta, so this will give you just the right amount of salt.

7. Garnish with fresh basil leaves and vegan Parmesan cheese.

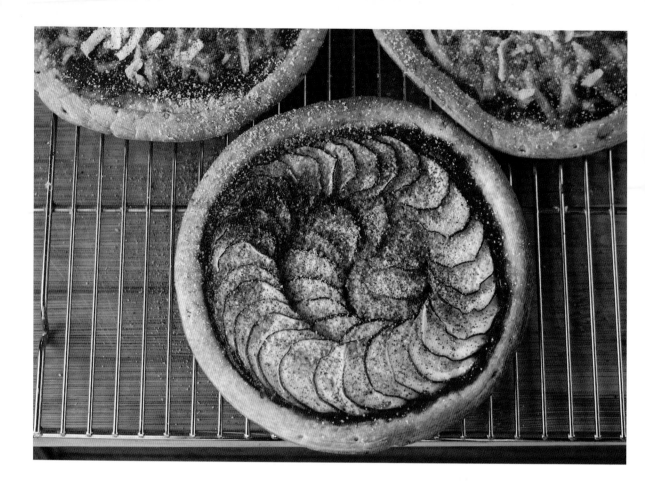

Our mother and grandmother were known for their homemade pizza. On any Sunday night, you could smell it baking in the house. Usually, they bought the square, thick pizza shells from the local bakery, but occasionally they made the dough from scratch. However, the most distinguishable feature of their pizza was the slightly sweet red sauce. It started with a base of Hunt's Tomato Sauce (Angie's favorite) and had a handful of ingredients that created this unique Italian specialty. Since Week 32 (see meal plan on page 57) is focused on pizza, you've got an excuse to pop a pie or two in the oven. This traditional version and our Broccoli Pizza that follows are two completely different styles for you to try; we're all about options.

TRADITIONAL "RED" PIZZA

Total Time: 25 minutes   Level: Easy   Serves: 16 slices

Ingredients

1 (8 oz.) can Hunt's Tomato Sauce

1 tsp. organic cane sugar

1 tsp. dried oregano

fresh ground black pepper, to taste

½ cup onion, finely diced (optional)

4 (8-inch) pizza crusts or 2 (16-inch) pizza
   crusts or French bread (optional)

Parmela Creamery Artisan Aged Nutmilk
   Cheese

veggies of your choice, for topping

Go Veggie! Vegan Grated Parmesan Style
   Topping

Directions

1. Preheat oven to 425°F.

2. Combine tomato sauce, sugar, oregano, black pepper, and onion to make sauce.

3. Top your favorite dough, shell, or split French bread and add your sauce and cheese.

4. Bake in the oven according to the directions on the pizza shell package. If using bread, bake until bread is toasted.

BROCCOLI PIZZA

Total Time: 30 minutes   Level: Easy   Servings: 16 slices

Ingredients

1 (12-inch) California Food Company Gluten Free Pizza Crust or prepared vegan pizza crust of your choice

2½ cups broccoli florets*

6 cloves garlic, minced

1 tbsp. olive oil

½ tsp. salt

fresh ground pepper

red pepper flakes, plus extra for garnish

Go Veggie! Vegan Grated Parmesan Style Topping, plus extra for garnish

4 oz. vegan mozzarella cheese such as Daiya Mozzarella Style Shreds or Miyoko's Kitchen Fresh Buffalo Mozzarella

Directions

1. Preheat oven to 425°F or according to pizza crust package directions.

2. Bring water to a simmer in a pot. Place a steamer basket in the pot and add broccoli florets. Steam broccoli until tender, 4 to 5 minutes. Set aside.

2. Sauté garlic on low heat in olive oil. Add broccoli florets, salt, pepper, and a large pinch of red pepper flakes.

3. Sprinkle the shredded vegan Parmesan and mozzarella cheeses on top of the pizza crust. Add the broccoli pieces on top so they are evenly distributed.

4. Bake pizza for 10 to 12 minutes or according to package directions.

5. Remove from oven and sprinkle generously with vegan Parmesan and red pepper flakes, if desired.

---

* Reserve the stems for another use, such as chopped in a soup or sautéed with garlic and olive oil.

Our Grandma Maira and mother had mastered the classic Neapolitan pizza for years. Crispy crust, sweet red sauce, toppings, what's not to like? Then a local vendor introduced a pizza made with one of the Sellani's favorite vegetables—broccoli. Game changer. The pure ingredients we enjoyed in our mother's sautéed broccoli and macaroni, with a quick swap of pasta for a pizza crust, created a delight that we loved as much as the classic red. Why didn't we think of this?

PIGS IN A BLANKET (STUFFED CABBAGE)

Total Time: 40 minutes   Level: Easy   Serving Size: 4

Our version of "Pigs in a Blanket," not to be confused with the more commonly known hotdog wrapped in dough, is a combination of protein, rice, and onions meticulously wrapped up in a cabbage leaf. While this historically Polish recipe varies a bit based on the sauce that is added, our mother and grandmothers used a tomato-based sauce. It's a perfect Week 14 recipe (see meal plan on page 57) to satisfy those beefy, comfort-food cravings.

Ingredients

1 large cabbage, core removed

1 cup Beefy Crumbles by Beyond Meat

1 tsp. fennel seeds, crushed between fingers

2 tsp. vegetable oil

¼ cup low-sodium vegetable broth

¾ cup white onion, minced

1 garlic clove, minced

1 tsp. salt

fresh ground black pepper, to taste

½ cup steamed brown rice

2 (14.1 oz.) cans Amy's Kitchen Chunky Tomato Bisque Soup

½ can of water measured in the soup container

1½ tbsp. organic sugar

Directions

1. In a large pot, boil the cabbage core side down. (Note: fill pot with enough water to cover half the cabbage—the thinner top leaves will steam while the tougher bottom leaves boil directly in the pot.) Periodically and carefully remove the outer leaves with cooking tongs as they start to cook and loosen. Repeat this process by removing leaves and returning the cabbage to the pot until you get to the small leaves in the center. You will need 8 leaves to make this recipe. (Reserve the leftover leaves for another use. They're great for soup or cabbage and noodles—a Polish delicacy).

(Continued)

222

2. The stem of the cabbage leaf can be tough, so with a small paring knife, trim the protruding stem on the leaf until it is reduced almost to the surface of leaf.

3. Sauté the beefy crumbles and fennel seeds in the oil until heated through, about 3 minutes.

4. Add the vegetable broth, onion, garlic, salt and pepper, rice, and ¼ cup of the tomato bisque soup and mix thoroughly. Remove from heat. Note: the onion will not be completely cooked through.

5. Put ¼ cup of the mixture onto the cabbage leaf. Wrap the rounded edge of the leaf over the mixture and roll forward, tucking in the sides while rolling until you have a little "package." Place the stuffed leaf seam side down in a large nonstick frying pan. Repeat until all the leaves are filled.

6. Mix the remaining tomato soup with water and sugar. Pour over the rolls in the pan. Heat and bring to boil. Then cover with a lid and let simmer for 20 minutes.

7. Serve the "piggies" with a generous portion of sauce.

Tip: Serve on a large scoop of mashed potatoes, or with crusty Italian bread to soak up the remaining sauce.

CHICK'N SCAMPI

Total Time: 25 minutes   Level: Easy   Serves: 4

Susan taught me how to make scampi because it was not something normally made in our household. She took it upon herself to learn it and makes a delicious vegan version that tastes like something you'd get in a fine dining restaurant. Week 27 (see meal plan on page 57) will bring out the vegan chicken lover in you, and so will this recipe, with the help of Gardein's high quality "chick'n" strips.

Ingredients

1½ tsp. EVOO

1 tbsp. minced garlic

2 tbsp. Earth Balance Natural Buttery Spread

1 package Gardein Teriyaki Chick'n Strips (discard sauce packet or use another time)

½ lb. white mushrooms, thickly sliced

½ cup Chardonnay or other white wine

1 tsp. salt

fresh cracked black pepper, to taste

¼ cup fresh squeezed lemon juice

¼ cup panko breadcrumbs

fresh flat leaf Italian parsley or finely cut chives, for garnish

Directions

1. In a large pan, heat the olive oil, garlic, and buttery spread on medium heat for approximately 2 minutes, being careful not to burn the garlic.

2. Sauté the chik'n strips in the olive oil mixture until they begin to turn golden brown, about 3 minutes.

3. Remove the chick'n strips from the pan and set aside. Add the mushrooms and wine to the pan and cook until they begin to soften, about 3-4 minutes. Continue to cook until wine reduces by about half.

(Continued)

4. Return the chicken to the pan. Add the salt, fresh pepper, lemon juice, and breadcrumbs. Continue to mix until everything is heated through. The breadcrumbs will soak up the liquid and become soft.

5. Garnish with fresh parsley or chives.

Tip: This can be served with a side of steamed vegetables or on top of angel hair pasta.

The fresh corn in Pennsylvania was a sure sign of summer. We ate ours simply, with butter and salt. But Southern California has some remarkable variations that incorporate the fresh and fiery flavors of neighboring Mexico. If you are used to eating your corn on the cob with butter and salt, you'll especially enjoy this variation in Week 36 (see meal plan on page 57) when choosing butter substitutes.

SoCal STREET CORN

Total Time: 35 minutes   Level: Easy   Serving Size: 2

SoCal Sauce Ingredients

1 red pepper

2 tbsp. So Delicious Dairy-Free Coconut Milk Yogurt Alternative

2 tbsp. fresh flat leaf parsley, chopped

juice of 1 lime

2 tbsp. fresh cilantro, chopped

½ tsp. cumin

1½ tsp. coriander

1–2 drops of Tapatío hot sauce

fresh cracked black pepper, to taste

Corn Ingredients

4 ears of fresh corn, husk and silk removed

1 tsp. salt

paprika, for garnish

fresh cilantro, chopped, for garnish

2 limes

SoCal Sauce Directions

1. Cut the red pepper in half lengthwise and roast by placing on a baking pan under the broiler until skin is charred, or char on the flame of a gas stove. When skin is blackened, put in paper bag for 15 minutes until cool. Remove from bag. Remove blackened skin and seed.

2. Add the flesh of the pepper with the cultured coconut milk, parsley, juice of 1 lime, cilantro, cumin, coriander, and hot sauce in food processor. Blend until fully incorporated and smooth.

Corn Directions

1. Bring large pot of water to boil. Add salt and corn. Cook for 3 to 5 minutes, until corn is crisp and tender. Remove from pot and discard water.

2. Drizzle SoCal Sauce on corn and top with paprika and cilantro.

3. Serve with lime wedges.

UNSTUFFED POBLANO PEPPER WITH MACADAMIA CHEESE

Total Time: 45 Minutes   Level: Medium   Serves: 4

Unstuffed Poblano Pepper Ingredients

4 Poblano peppers

salt and pepper, to taste

½ cup black beans

½ cup corn kernels

juice of ½ lime

generous pinch of cumin

2 tbsp. cilantro, chopped, plus extra for garnish

1 small tomato, seeded and diced

2 tbsp. red onion, diced, plus extra for garnish

1 corn tortilla, sliced in 2-inch "matchsticks"

small amount of neutral cooking oil

paprika, to taste

Macadamia Cheese Ingredients

¾ cup macadamia nuts, soaked for 4 hours or overnight, rinsed and drained

¼ cup water

2 tbsp. lemon juice

¼ tsp. salt

generous pinch garlic granules or fresh clove of garlic, minced

⅛ cup nutritional yeast

Unstuffed Poblano Pepper Directions

1. Roast the peppers by putting them under a broiler until skins are charred and blackened. (If you have a gas oven, you can heat them directly on the flame using metal tongs.) Transfer them directly from the oven into a paper bag. Fold the bag closed to allow peppers to steam.

2. When cool, remove the stems, skins, and seeds from the peppers. Dice peppers and add a bit of salt and pepper. Set aside and keep warm. (Warning: do not touch your eyes after handling the peppers or seeds.)

(Continued)

3. In a separate pan, mix beans and corn with lime juice, cumin, cilantro, chopped tomato, red onion, salt, and pepper. Mix over low heat. Set aside and keep warm.

4. Heat the matchstick-cut tortilla in a small nonstick pan using a scant bit of oil. Stir, getting oil on the tortilla, then add salt, pepper, and paprika. Continue to cook until the matchsticks are firm with a little crunch. Set aside.

Macadamia Cheese Directions

1. Mix all ingredients in small food processor until completely blended. The cheese will resemble ricotta and will have a little granularity from the nuts. If you want a smoother cheese, you can add more water. Set aside.

To Serve

1. Use a 2" tall ring to stack the ingredients, or simply place each layer on four serving plates. This can be very rustic.

2. First place the peppers on the bottom of the ring or plate.

3. Add the bean and corn mixture for the second layer—save a few tablespoons for the top.

4. Add the cheese for third layer, followed by a little more bean mixture.

5. Top with the crunchy tortilla strips.

6. Garnish with additional chopped red onion or cilantro, if desired.

PARMESAN-STYLE STUFFED ARTICHOKES

Total Time: 90 minutes   Level: Medium   Serves: 3

This unusual and delicious vegetable was introduced to us as children by our Grandma Maira. We were young enough not to question the odd method of eating the leaves (by pulling them over our lower teeth), but old enough to revel in the exhilaration of that fork-tender heart. Many artichoke recipes involve removing most of the leaves, but you will find that they are truly delectable when prepared stuffed à la Grandma Maira.

Ingredients

1 cup panko breadcrumbs

¼ cup Go Veggie! Grated Parmesan Style Topping

¼ tsp. garlic powder

½ tsp. salt

fresh ground black pepper

3 (1 pound) extra-large artichokes

1½ tbsp. EVOO

2–4 cups of water

1 lemon, cut into wedges

Directions

1. Mix breadcrumbs, Parmesan topping, garlic powder, salt, and pepper in large bowl. Stir with fork until thoroughly incorporated.

2. Cut the stem off each artichoke at the base. The choke should be able to stand up on the base without tipping over. Cut about ½ to ¾ inch off the top of each choke to get the majority of pointed tips. Use scissors to cut sharp tips off the remaining leaves.

3. Starting at the lowest leaves, use a spoon to force open each leaf while simultaneously pouring the breadcrumb mixture so that it lands at the base of the leaf. Continue this process, rotating the choke while depositing the mixture deep into the base of the leaves, working your way to the top of the choke and the most tightly packed leaves. You may not

(Continued)

230

be able to get the spoon into the tight center of the choke. Instead, sprinkle a spoonful of mixture on top of the choke. Drizzle ½ tbsp. EVOO over each choke.

4. Place a steamer basket at the base of a large pot with simmering water beneath the basket. Use 2 to 4 cups, depending on the size of your pot; the water should not touch the chokes. Steam the chokes until an outer leaf can be pulled out easily. This should take 55 to 65 minutes, depending on the size of the chokes. Continue to check the chokes and add water to the bottom of the pot to prevent it from completely evaporating—do not pour water on top of chokes.

5. When thoroughly steamed, remove the choke from the pot. Serve with lemon wedges and fresh cracked black pepper.

6. To eat the choke, simply pull off leaves, one at a time, starting at the base. There is no need to dip the leaf into a sauce, since the stuffing will give it plenty of flavor. Put the leaf in your mouth, holding one end. Pull the leaf through your closed teeth to eat the breadcrumb mixture and artichoke pulp. Discard the leaf.

Tip: When you eat all the leaves, you will arrive at delicious heart of the artichoke. Scrape the "choke" off of the heart with the flat side of a fork and discard. You can add additional salt and pepper or a squeeze of lemon, if desired. Cut the heart into bite-sized pieces and enjoy. They will be tender and flavorful. This is the reward at the end of the artichoke.

SPAGHETTI SQUASH WITH GARLIC, TOMATO & BASIL

Total Time: 90 minutes   Level: Easy   Serves: 4

Susan turned me on to spaghetti squash because I can eat pasta three times a day and really wanted an alternative. At first, I didn't believe that it could actually satisfy like pasta, but it's an impressive substitute.

Ingredients

1 (3–3½ pound) spaghetti squash

2 tbsp. olive oil

¼ tsp. salt, to taste

fresh ground black pepper, to taste

4 cloves garlic, minced

2 cups chopped heirloom tomatoes

4 tbsp. lemon juice

1 cup fresh basil, ribboned, plus extra for garnish

Directions

1. Heat oven to 450°F. Cut spaghetti squash in half, lengthwise. Take extreme caution in doing this. The squash is hard and you will need a sharp knife.

2. Scoop out seeds and discard. Drizzle each half with ½ tbsp. olive oil and sprinkle with salt and pepper. Place cut side up on a baking pan lined with aluminum foil. Bake for 50 minutes or until a knife can be easily inserted into the squash.

3. Scrape the inside of each half with a fork, pulling the stringy pulp from the squash. Put in bowl.

4. Sauté garlic in 1 tbsp. olive oil. Add squash, tomatoes, lemon juice, salt, and pepper and mix until heated through. Remove from heat. Add basil and heat again.

5. Place in serving dishes. Top with additional fresh basil, for garnish.

TACOS VERDES

Total Time: 15 minutes   Level: Easy   Serves: 4

Even hardcore carnivores will devour these!

Ingredients

1 (12 oz.) jar marinated artichoke hearts, lightly rinsed and drained

½ tbsp. vegetable oil

1 cup white mushrooms, sliced

¼–½ cup water

1 cup baby spinach, tightly packed

salt and pepper, to taste

4 corn tortillas

½ avocado, cubed

½ cup salsa verde (tomatillo salsa)

¼ cup cilantro, chopped

1 lime (optional)

Directions

1. Sauté artichoke hearts in oil on medium heat until heated through.

2. Add mushrooms and continue to cook until mushrooms are soft, about 3 to 5 minutes.

3. Add a little water to create steam and prevent from sticking.

4. Add spinach until wilted, about one minute.

5. Add salt and pepper to taste.

6. Heat corn tortillas using gas flame of oven, or if you have an electric oven, heat them on a nonstick pan until warm.

7. Add artichoke mixture to tortillas.

8. Top with avocado, salsa verde, cilantro, and squeeze of lime, if desired.

LENTIL SHEPHERD'S PIE

Total Time: 50 minutes   Level: Medium   Serves: 4–6

We love lentils and use them to replace the meat in this Shepherd's pie, which is piled high with veggies and mashed potatoes. It's comfort food plus fiber—the best of both worlds. Week 48 (see meal plan on page 57) recommends a turkey-free Thanksgiving, and this dish would make a perfect holiday entrée.

Ingredients:

1 cups green lentils

3 cups water

1 tbsp. salt

½ (6 oz.) onion, uncut

1 garlic clove

2 bay leaves

2 lbs. russet potatoes, cubed

1 cup Silk Unsweetened Almond Milk

1 tbsp. Bragg nutritional yeast

1 flax egg*

1 (16 oz.) bag frozen peas, corn, and carrots

salt and fresh ground pepper, to taste

paprika, to taste

1 cup flat leaf parsley, chopped

Directions:

1. Run lentils under running water and check for small stones or other particles—these are rare, but worth checking for.

2. Bring 2 cups water to a boil. Once boiling, add salt, onion, garlic, bay leaves, and lentils. Bring heat to a low boil and cook an additional 25 to 30 minutes until lentils are tender. Most of the water will be absorbed. Drain any remaining liquid and set aside.

3. While cooking lentils, bring 1 cup water to boil in another large pot.

4. Add potatoes and bring to slow boil, cooking until soft enough to mash, about 12 minutes.

5. Mash the potatoes with milk, nutritional yeast, and flax egg.

6. Add salt and pepper to taste.

7. Cook frozen peas, corn, and carrots according to package directions.

8. Add salt and pepper to taste.

(Continued)

To Serve:

1. Add lentils to bottom of casserole dish, spread evenly to cover bottom.

2. Add vegetables on top, spread evenly to cover lentils.

3. Add mashed potatoes on top, spread evenly to cover top of dish.

4. Sprinkle with paprika and place about 6 inches under oven broiler until potatoes start to feel slightly crisp to the touch.

5. Remove from oven. Top with chopped parsley and serve.

---

* Grind whole flax seeds in high speed blender, then measure 1 tbsp. Mix 1 tbsp. of the flax meal with 3 tbsp. water, and chill in fridge for 15 minutes while preparing other ingredients.

GRANDMA'S STUFFED PASTA SHELLS

Total Time: 65 minutes   Level: Medium   Serves: 22 Stuffed Shells (4–5 servings)

As a family who happily dined on pasta multiple times per week, our mother was always looking for new ways to keep her meals creative and interesting. Historically, pasta shells are filled with cheese, but the Sellanis may have been the only Italians on the planet who didn't like ricotta cheese. So Angie innovatively used the components for Grandma Sellani's meat and spinach raviolis, and filled pasta shells for a new and exciting way to serve them. They were a huge hit. Try these in Week 14 (see meal plan on page 57): we promise you won't miss the beef.

Ingredients

1 (12 oz.) box jumbo pasta shells

1 (10 oz.) package frozen spinach

2 tbsp. EVOO

¾ cup onion, finely diced

2 cloves garlic, minced

2 cups Beef-Free Crumbles by Beyond Meat

¼ tsp. ground cinnamon

¼ tsp. ground cloves

¾ tsp. salt

5–6 grinds fresh black pepper

1 (22 oz.) jar Classico Tomato & Basil Sauce

Go Veggie! Brand Vegan Parmesan cheese

fresh basil leaves, cut into ribbons

Directions

1. Preheat oven to 350°F. Bring a large pot of water to boil.

2. Boil 26 pasta shells; there will be some leftover. You will only end up filling about 22, but some will break in the process of cooking. Cook according to package directions—do not overcook. It's better to have them a little "al dente" (firm to the bite) because you will be baking them in the oven later.

(Continued)

3. Place spinach under faucet. Thaw with warm running water until thawed. Squeeze out excess water with hands. Measure one cup of spinach.

4. Heat olive oil in skillet on medium to low heat. Add onion and sauté, stirring constantly until onion is translucent, about 4 minutes. Add minced garlic and continue to stir just until garlic is heated through—be careful not to burn the garlic or it will taste bitter.

5. Add beefy crumbles and spinach and continue to sauté until entire mixture is heated throughout. Add cinnamon, cloves, salt, and pepper and mix.

6. When shells are done cooking, carefully drain them by pouring into a colander or removing them with a slotted spoon. Place them individually on a plate to ensure they do not stick together.

7. Let the shells cool enough for you to handle them. Fill each shell with beefy mixture. The easiest way to do this is to scoop the mixture with an ice cream scoop. Stuff the shell with about ¼ cup of the mixture so it's nice and plump. This will make approximately 22 stuffed shells.

8. Pour half the jar of sauce into a baking pan until the bottom is covered. Place stuffed shells in the pan side-by-side, until all shells are in the pan. Pour the remainder of the sauce over the shells.

9. Cover in foil and bake for 30 minutes.

10. Garnish with Parmesan cheese and fresh basil leaves.

MASHED SWEET POTATO TACOS WITH CILANTRO RICE AND MACADAMIA SOUR CREAM

Total Time: 35 minutes   Level: Medium   Serves: 2 (2 tacos each)

Susan and I didn't truly experience tacos until we had them in Southern California. There are so many variations and this one definitely delivers. The taste of fresh squeezed lime and sweet potato is divine. The red onions, green cilantro, bright red tomatoes, crunchy purple cabbage, and velvety avocado make this dish a flavorful color fest.

Macadamia Sour Cream Ingredients:

1 cup macadamia nuts soaked in water for at least 2 hours, rinsed and drained

¾ cup water

¼ cup lemon juice

½ tsp. lemon zest

½ tsp. salt

1 clove garlic

2 tbsp. grape-seed oil

Taco Ingredients:

1½ cups (1 large) sweet potato, diced, or frozen sweet potato cubes

¼–½ cup almond milk

salt and pepper, to taste

1 cup brown rice, cooked according to package directions*

2 tbsp. cilantro, chopped

1 tbsp. lime juice

4 corn tortillas, warmed in the oven or in a pan

red onion, chopped, for garnish

tomato, chopped, for garnish

fresh cilantro, chopped for garnish

purple cabbage, finely shredded, for garnish

avocado slices, for garnish

Macadamia Sour Cream (recipe below)

lime wedges, for garnish

(Continued)

238

Macadamia Sour Cream Directions:

1. Mix all ingredients in small food processor except oil. When ingredients are fully blended, slowly pour oil in steady stream until mixture is fully blended.

Taco Directions:

1. Place the sweet potatoes in boiling water and cook until tender enough to mash, about 15 minutes. If using frozen sweet potato, steam according to package directions. Drain potatoes and place in bowl. Add almond milk a little at a time and mash with fork or potato masher until you achieve the consistency of mashed potatoes. Only use enough milk to make them creamy, not soupy. Add salt and pepper to taste.

2. Warm the rice by heating in a sauce pan. Add cilantro, juice of lime, and salt and pepper, if needed. Set aside.

3. Place mashed sweet potato mixture on each tortilla.

4. Place rice mixture on top of potato mixture.

5. Add red onion, tomato, cilantro, cabbage, avocado, Macadamia Sour Cream, and lime and serve.

---

*To save time, use leftover brown rice or quinoa.

INSPIRATIONAL VEGAN

MARTY KRUTOLOW

Owner, Marty's V Burgers

An Unlikely Vegan

"I used to smoke a couple packs of cigarettes a day and was looking for an excuse to keep smoking while doing something good for my body. I gave up meat and chicken and traded them in for mozzarella and Doritos," Marty Krutlow recalls. While Marty's first steps on the plant-based path might not sound like the ideal entrance to a healthier lifestyle, everyone's journey is unique. It doesn't matter *where* we start, it matters *that* we start. And sometimes, how we start serves an important purpose in our own evolution and our ability to genuinely influence those around us.

Regardless of your current vices—smoking, junk food, processed food, red meat—you can start to improve your situation by simply taking that important first step in the right direction. And Marty did just that. Today, he is inviting others to join him by making vegan food that is both delicious and accessible.

Roots in the Non-Vegan World

Like many of us over age forty, Marty grew up in a time when vegan living was not a buzzword, let alone a movement. He recalls, "My grandfather was a New York butcher and my grandmother used to surprise me by putting a hot dog in the meatloaf." What kid wouldn't love that? As an adult, Marty worked on boats in Brooklyn where he says "I killed my fair share of fish."

Marty had experimented with a vegetarian life for eighteen years, being influenced by his cousin who said that omitting meat would help get a flatter belly, and his girlfriend who had given him a book on vegetarianism. He started becoming interested in researching food and nutrition. He even started experimenting with cooking and making his own seitan (pronounced SAY-tan), a vegan meat substitute created from wheat protein. At the time, Marty's roommate was an open-minded omnivore willing to try anything as long as it tasted good. So Marty had a receptive audience of one to taste-test his experimental culinary creations. Those experiments would ultimately pay off.

Marty started to research the food he was putting into his body. "You can't do research on what you should be eating without seeing what's going on in the food world," he says. "I was also a commercial pilot at the time, and my desire to eat vegan was more difficult on the road. When you are part of a crew, you eat with the people you fly with, so I would be at a restaurant with everyone else, where there were no vegan options. I wanted to avoid animal products, but then I'd be at Applebee's ordering the shrimp Caesar salad."

As the years progressed, Marty was eating so little meat and dairy, he started to identify with being a vegan. "Of the ninety meals I ate a month, maybe two weren't vegan," he recalls. "But I read a column by a Philadelphia food writer who said that if you're still eating animal products, you should stop calling yourself a vegan. I sat with that for a while and

I realized that eating meat and dairy wasn't important to me. Slowly but surely I dropped all animal foods. I started having discussions in my head, 'Why can't I eat oysters?' I didn't think they felt anything, but what if they did? I really didn't know, so I gave them up. The last decision was about honey. I don't really have the patience to get involved with why you can't eat honey, so I just decided, if I'm in it for a penny, I'm in it for a pound." And with that final confirmation, Marty was a true vegan. That was eight years ago.

Filling the Gap: Vegan Fast Food

Marty speaks with the business sense and creativity of an entrepreneur. Perhaps it was the road trips during his days as a pilot that gave him an appreciation for the difficulty of dining out as a vegan—and the inspiration to do something about it. His first venture to help others find plant-based menus started with a blog called *Marty's Flying Vegan Review*. "I reviewed meals I had all over the world. I also watched about fifteen thousand hours of the Food Channel and realized there were

restaurants making amazing vegan food with no people in them and restaurants making mediocre food with lines around the block. I knew that if I had convenient, fast food vegan restaurants in my own neighborhood, I would eat there every day."

Vegan Burgers Even a Carnivore Could Love

Marty is on a mission to destroy the myth that vegans eat "rabbit food." About three years ago, he gave up flying and developed a menu of vegan fast food items for local food festivals, pop-up events, and concerts to test his hearty, "meaty" products. "We wanted to see if this was something we could make work in the real world, not just catering to vegans. We were successful at New York's Evergreen Food Festival, but what if we were just on a street in New York City?" Marty soon found out when he hosted a booth in Manhattan's Bryant Park to the general public. The verdict was in—omnivores and vegans alike loved his food, and Marty's concept of a vegan fast food brick and mortar store began to evolve.

"Part of our mission statement is to have quick and affordable food," he explains. Basically, a vegan version of McDonalds. He adds "While there are vegan food chains like Veggie Grill, they still have a longer wait time." Marty's need for speed combined with a demand for quality products can fill a void in today's restaurant space. "Our target market is the person who wants a healthy lunch but has no time to wait for a table. We're trying to make this affordable and fast," a promise that Marty keeps regularly with burgers flying off the grill in less than two minutes and starting at just six dollars.

Marty's V Burger is still in its early stages but showing promise as he continues to gain an opposable "thumbs up" from carnivores and vegans alike throughout New York City. "We have just recently signed a lease and are moving forward on it. We're not branding ourselves as health food but the food is healthy by default because there's no cholesterol." With a base of seitan, black beans, and rice, Marty's burgers have a hearty, satisfying core. Variations include the Shroom Steakhouse Burger topped with vegan mozzarella and the Crabby Patty with Cajun Tartar sauce. The menu also has Drum Stix with Buffalo sauce and Bleu Cheez. No rabbit food here.

"We created the menu with flavor in mind, keeping the price point down. We're not making artisanal burgers for fifteen dollars,

we're looking for a much lower price point."
While Marty jokes "I'm sure my mother would
be proud that I have a job flipping burgers"
he is truly the visionary and rainmaker for the
company and enjoys business operations over
food preparation. He is looking for investors
who are interested in the concept of a green or
ethical investment portfolio and wants to grow
the brand nationwide. That growth requires
selecting locations in densely populated areas
to support a high volume business model.

"We did a round of loans with friends and
family lending us money. We could have self-
funded but we went on a handshake to prove
that we were credit-worthy. We're completing
the ninety-day cycle and repaying those
loans to establish a credit reference." In a
month, Marty will go back for another round
of loans. His ninety-day funding strategy has
proven to early investors that Marty's word is
as good as his burgers.

No one knows the siren call of comfort
food better than Marty. It's how his journey
began. It helped him create more affordable
and tastier food than the unhealthy Doritos
and mozzarella of his early years as a vegan.
His unlikely entry into the plant-based world
served as the perfect platform to create and
share the concept of the comfort food we all
crave with a healthier, vegan twist. After all,
if you're going to win over a carnivore, it's
more likely to happen with a burger than a

salad. It's quite possible that one of Marty's V
Burgers is exactly what people need to start
them on their own path to plant-based living.

Questions to Consider

1. Do you have favorite comfort foods that
   are preventing you from going vegan,
   such as cheese, pizza, burgers, or fried
   chicken? Have you tried vegan versions
   of these, including brands like Amy's,
   Gardein, and Beyond Meat?

2. Have you made efforts to go vegan but
   find it difficult when eating out? Have
   you ever used apps like Happy Cow to
   find vegan restaurants in your area?

3. Do you know of at least one or two
   restaurants near your home or work
   that have vegan options?

4. How difficult is it for you to find a
   vegan option from a menu when you
   are dining with non-vegans?

5. If eating vegan was easier simply
   because there were more affordable
   vegan restaurants available to you,
   how much would that influence your
   eating habits?

BONUS RECIPE

MARTY'S TOFU SCRAMBLE

Marty's recipe is more of a descriptive one rather than a list of ingredients and directions. That's just the way he rolls. Here is the recipe in Marty's own words and honest New York style:

My go-to recipe for breakfast is a stalwart of the vegan world: a tofu scramble. I'm not going to give you quantities because a) I think it's pretty silly to measure a cup of mushrooms or a cup of sliced onions, and b) you can do anything you want with cooking. You hate mushrooms, don't put any in. You like garlic, add two more cloves.

The most important thing is to learn how long things take to cook and put them in earlier or later in the process. I have bags of frozen mushrooms and mixed peppers in the freezer as a staple, and they're just as handy and good as fresh. Also, you need to learn if you like a lot of salt or pepper and how much that is. Start with a little and taste your dish often, and season again as you go along.

I also chop and add as I go, but I've made the recipe often enough and have gotten pretty good with a knife, so that by the time the oil in the pan is up to temp I have the onion cut. If you're new to this recipe, you should have everything in place before you start to eliminate the stress of not having something ready while something else burns.

"Meat" or tofu: If you use vegan sausages, you'll want to cook them up and put a little sear on them. If you just throw them in later they will come out "meh." Nothing wrong with that, but better if they have a little finish on them. Take them out, put them aside, and throw them in before you're done with the dish.

I've also made this dish with firm tofu, soft tofu, and pressed tofu and I don't think it really makes all that big a difference. If you press the tofu, you'll have a lot less liquid in the pan and will avoid steaming everything instead of sautéing it. (I long ago gave up the stacking of dishes and cans on top of a towel-wrapped block of tofu after the tenth time they went crashing over, so now I use a great product, TofuXpress, that does it for me.)

Onion: Chop or slice ½ onion or 2, it's up to you. Turn pan to medium heat and add a little oil. Add the onions and let cook for a few minutes. Add the onions first so the garlic won't burn.

Garlic: Smash some garlic with a knife and mince it up. Add that.

Mushrooms: Slice up a box of fresh mushrooms or throw in some frozen. If you use frozen ingredients, you'll need to crank up the heat a little bit as the frozen items will lower the pan temp. Make sure you remember to lower it back to medium.

Salt: Mushrooms take a little time to cook down, so add some salt here to extract the water from them. If you have fresh leftovers, slice them up and toss them in.

Peppers: Throw in a handful of tri-colored peppers from the freezer. While those cook, squeeze the pressed tofu into a bowl, using your hands, so it looks like scrambled eggs.

Spices: Add salt (black salt is better as it has a sulphur taste, just like eggs), pepper, turmeric, and some vegetable broth powder and mush it all together.

"Cheese": Toss the tofu in along with 1 handful . . . or 2 . . . or 3 of Daiya Cheddar Style Shreds. I also use a couple slices of Vegan Chao Cheese Slices. Whatever floats your boat. Or doesn't. You make this recipe yours. Dairy cheese often melts fast because of the temperature of the food, but I've found that you need a lot more heat to melt vegan cheese, so I usually stir the mixture until it gets gloppy. (I have said many times that I love gloppy food). Add the sausages and badda bing badda boom, you got ya self a tofu scramble!

CHAPTER 13

Desserts

"When I was young, I admired clever people. Now that I am old, I admire kind people."
—Abraham Joshua Heschel

BANANA COCONUT CUPCAKES

Total Time: 40 minutes   Level: Easy   Serves: 12 cupcakes

Dessert isn't something our mother made every night, and that makes sense. View dessert as a special treat and take the time to make dessert from scratch. A perfectly light frosting is provided by So Delicious Coco Whip, recommended in Week 16 (see meal plan on page 57).

Ingredients

12 cupcake wrappers

12-cup muffin tin

1½ cups unbleached, all-purpose flour

1 tsp. baking powder

1 tsp. baking soda

½ tsp. salt

3 ripe bananas

¾ cup agave nectar

1 tbsp. freshly ground flax meal*

⅓ cup applesauce

1 container So Delicious Brand Coco Whip Topping

dried, unsweetened coconut flakes

fresh, edible flower petals, for garnish

Organic confectioners' sugar, for garnish

Directions

1. Preheat oven to 375°F. Place cupcake wrappers into the wells of the muffin tin.

2. Mix flour, baking powder, baking soda, and salt in a bowl. Set aside.

3. In a separate bowl, mix bananas, agave nectar, flax mixture, and applesauce. Slowly add in flour mixture until all ingredients are incorporated.

4. Evenly distribute mixture into the wells of the muffin tin. Bake for 17 to 20 minutes or until toothpick inserted into the center comes out clean.

5. Let muffins cool approximately 10 minutes. Top with a dollop of Coco Whip, coconut flakes, confectioners' sugar, and edible flower petals, if desired.

---

* Grind whole flax seeds in high speed blender, then measure 1 tbsp. mixed with 3 tbsp. water, and chill in fridge for 15 minutes while preparing other ingredients.

AUNT LENA'S BLUEBERRY TARTS

Total Time: 30 minutes   Level: Easy   Serves: 4

Our Aunt Lena makes a wonderful blueberry pie with a combination of cooked and fresh berries, and a premade pie crust. This version uses a homemade no-cook crust made with buttery pecans and apricots, providing most of the sweetness of the tart. The blueberry filling has no sugar added, providing a perfect tart complement to the crust. This recipe is a perfect Week 39 option (see meal plan on page 57) when you're craving a piece of pie.

Pecan Crust Ingredients

1½ cups pecans

1 cup dried apricots

2 tbsp. coconut oil

Filling Ingredients

2 pints fresh blueberries

1 tbsp. cornstarch

1 tbsp. water

4 tbsp. organic confectioners' sugar

8 small, fresh basil leaves

Pecan Crust Directions:

1. Pulse pecans, apricots, and coconut oil in a food processor until you create a fine sticky mixture.

2. Press the mixture into four tart pans (with removable bottoms) If you do not have a tartlet pan, you can use glass ramekins. Save about 2 tablespoons of mixture as a garnish.

3. Put tart pans in fridge.

Filling Directions:

1. Put 1 pint of blueberries in a sauce pan. Heat for 10 minutes on low to medium heat, stirring regularly with a wooden spoon. Heat will start to break down blueberries. Some will

(Continued)

pop on their own. Press and stir the blueberries to further help the breakdown. After 10 minutes, a chunky "sauce" will form that looks like a traditional blueberry pie filling.

2. Add 1 tablespoon cornstarch and 1 tablespoon water. Cook to a slow boil. Stir completely. Reduce heat to low.

3. Add the other pint of blueberries and mix thoroughly for another 3 minutes.

To Serve

1. Add the blueberry mixture to the refrigerated tartlet pans.

2. Let cool in fridge for at least four hours or overnight.

3. Sprinkle with reserved pecan crust, confectioners' sugar and basil leaves.

Tip: Store the "bowl" of the ice cream maker in your freezer so it's ready to use any time. This has more of a tart flavor, similar to frozen yogurt.

BLACKBERRY "NICE" CREAM

Our Pennsylvania summers were short and sweet, just like this blackberry soft serve nice cream, which will disappear as quickly as you can make it. The creaminess comes from full fat coconut milk, leaving the cow completely out of the equation (that's why it's *nice* cream). Week 17 (see meal plan on page 57) is a great time to try this frozen treat and experiment with your new version of ice cream.

Ingredients

1 cup frozen banana*, sliced

6 oz. fresh blackberries or raspberries

1 can Thai Kitchen Organic Coconut Milk

½ cup agave nectar

1 tsp. pure vanilla extract

pinch salt

slivered almonds, for garnish

unsweetened coconut flakes, for garnish

Directions

1. In a high-power blender, blend all ingredients except almonds and coconut flakes.

2. Put mixture into ice cream maker for 20 minutes. Add additional berries in the last 5 minutes of processing. Stop the mixture while it is still creamy, like soft serve.

3. Scoop into dessert dishes. Top with almonds and coconut flakes, and enjoy immediately.

---

* Freeze in plastic bag overnight.

APPLESAUCE CAKE
WITH CINNAMON GLAZE

Total Time: 60 minutes   Level: Easy   Serves: 8 slices

Our mom used to make a simple applesauce cake that was rustic, sweet, and moist. We've added an optional cinnamon glaze, but this cake is moist enough to eat plain.

Cinnamon Glaze Ingredients

¼ cup agave nectar

½ cup So Delicious Cultured Coconut Milk

¾ tbsp. lemon juice

¼ tsp. pure vanilla extract

⅛ tsp. cinnamon

Applesauce Cake Ingredients

½–1 tbsp. coconut oil

1½ cups oat flour

1 tsp. baking powder

1 tsp. baking soda

½ tsp. salt

1 tbsp. freshly ground flax meal*

1½ cups unsweetened applesauce

¾ cup agave nectar

½ cup walnuts or pecans, chopped

Cinnamon Glaze Directions

1. Mix all ingredients until fully incorporated. Keep in fridge until ready to use.

Apple Bread Recipe Directions

1. Preheat oven to 350°F. Use coconut oil to grease a 4 x 8-inch loaf pan.

2. Mix oat flour, baking powder, baking soda, and salt until fully incorporated.

(Continued)

---

* Grind whole flax seeds in high-speed blender, then measure 1 tbsp. mixed with 3 tbsp. water, and chill in fridge for 15 minutes while preparing other ingredients.

3. Add flax meal mixture, applesauce, and agave nectar to the oat mixture and blend with electric mixer or wire whisk until fully incorporated. Do not overmix. Fold in nuts by hand, if using.

4. Fill pan with batter and bake for 45 to 50 minutes or until toothpick inserted into center of cake comes out clean.

5. Remove cake from oven and let cool for 5 minutes. Gently remove cake from pan by turning pan upside down on top of a clean kitchen towel and shaking gently until cake comes out. If the cake does not come out easily, you may have to run a butter knife around the inside edge of the pan to loosen. Slice into 8 (1-inch) slices.

6. Drizzle slices with cinnamon glaze and chopped walnuts.

MOM'S CHOCOLATE CHIP COOKIES

Total Time: 30 minutes   Level: Easy   Serves: 24 cookies

Our mother was known for her outstanding cooking, but specialized in only a handful of baked goods. Her Toll House cookies were at the top of the list and a family favorite. Our mother followed the standard recipe; but, like everything she made, she always added a heaping portion of walnuts and love. That must have been why they tasted so good.

Ingredients

1¼ cups unbleached, all-purpose flour

½ tsp. baking soda

½ tsp. salt

1 tbsp. flax egg*

½ cup unsweetened applesauce

¼ cup agave nectar

¾ cup Sugar In The Raw

½ tsp. pure vanilla extract

¾ cup dairy-free chocolate chips (we like Sunspire 42% cacao semi-sweet chips)

½ cup chopped walnuts

almond, cashew, or coconut milk

Directions:

1. Preheat the oven to 375°F.

2. Combine flour, baking soda, salt, and flax mixture in a bowl. Mix until combined.

3. Using electric mixer, blend applesauce, agave, sugar, and vanilla extract. While still mixing, add flour mixture ½ cup at a time until thoroughly blended.

4. By hand, stir in chocolate chips and walnuts.

5. Drop mixture by rounded tablespoons onto a nonstick baking sheet.

(Continued)

---

* Grind whole flax seeds in high speed blender, then measure 1 tbsp. Mix 1 tbsp. of the flax meal with 3 tbsp. water, and chill in fridge for 15 minutes while preparing other ingredients.

6. Bake for 9 to 11 minutes until cookies start to turn golden brown. Remove from oven and let cool on wire racks for 2 minutes. Then carefully remove cookies from the baking sheet. These cookies will come up a little lighter and spongier than the traditional recipe.

7. Serve with a cold glass of almond, cashew, or coconut milk.

Tip: Omit the cacao and add an extra ½ tsp. of vanilla to make vanilla rocky road.

ROCKIER ROAD "NICE" CREAM

Total Time: 30 minutes   Level: Easy   Serves: 1 quart

Some of us take our rocky road seriously. We're not likely to settle for store bought brands that skimp on the marshmallows. We're not interested in treasure hunts for scant pieces of walnut. We want big chunks of goodies in every bite. But first, let's talk marshmallows. If you haven't had Sweet & Sara Vegan Marshmallows, you haven't had marshmallows. They're not only the best vegan marshmallows available, they're the best marshmallows anywhere. No cornstarchy coating on these perfectly cubed confections; just pure goodness.

Ingredients

2 cans full-fat coconut milk

3 tbsp. cacao powder, plus extra for garnish

¾ cup agave nectar

½ tsp. pure vanilla extract

pinch salt

4 ice cubes

¾ cup walnut halves, coarsely chopped

½ cup vegan chocolate chips, (we like Sunspire 42% cacao semi-sweet chips)

8 Sweet & Sara Vegan Marshmallows

Directions:

1. In high-powered blender, mix coconut milk, cacao powder, agave, vanilla extract, salt, and ice cubes until thoroughly combined.

2. Pour mixture through a mesh strainer into the ice cream maker and turn on. Read directions for your ice cream maker to familiarize yourself with proper usage.

3. Mixture will start to get soft within about 15 minutes. Keep an eye on it.

4. When mixture resembles soft serve, start adding walnuts, chocolate chips, and marshmallows while machine is still churning. Alternate walnuts, chips, and marshmallows for even distribution.

5. Serve immediately and sprinkle with cacao powder, if desired.

INSPIRATIONAL VEGANS

RICK AND CAROLYN SOLAN

Owners, Prestige Chem Dry Cleaners

In 2005, while caddying for his son at a golf tournament, Rick Solan picked up what looked like just another magazine from a display case. He didn't notice what was on the cover, but what was inside got his immediate attention—startling photos of a poultry factory farm. Rick soon realized he was reading a publication produced by PETA (People for the Ethical Treatment of Animals[33]).

Disturbed by the images he saw, Rick called his wife, Carolyn, to share what he had experienced. After doing additional research, Rick and Carolyn decided to become vegetarian. They omitted meat from their diets, but still ate dairy products. Rick recalls, "We weren't on a healthy lifestyle. We still ate pizzas, lots of cheese, and ice cream." But that lifestyle ultimately changed.

A Diagnosis, A New Way of Life

Six years later, Rick's doctor gave him the news. Rick had a bicuspid aortic valve that needed to be replaced. About 2 percent of the population have bicuspid aortic valve disease (BAVD). While the cause is not completely clear, the defective valve is often present at birth[34].

It was a serious situation, Rick recalls. "I met with the doctor who went over what he was going to do during surgery. It wasn't pleasant. That same evening, we

---

[33]People for the Ethical Treatment of Animals, www.peta.org

[34]http://my.clevelandclinic.org/services/heart/disorders/heart-valve-disease/bicuspid_aortic_valve_disease

260

saw a commercial that Bill Clinton's doctor was going to be on CNN to discuss how he was curing Clinton's heart disease."

Health Inspiration from a Former President

The CNN story was a turning point for Rick and Carolyn. President Clinton ultimately chose a vegan diet to maintain his health *after* his two heart procedures—a quadruple bypass surgery to restore blood flow to his heart in 2004, and two stents to open one of the veins in 2010.[35]

Rick recalls, "It got me interested in the possibility of reversing my heart disease to avoid open heart surgery. Even though I learned that Clinton's heart disease was not the same as my heart valve problem, I also learned that a vegan diet could eliminate health problems associated with the standard American diet (SAD). I had never heard of SAD prior to this. My wife and I were both overweight and out of shape, and I was going to have heart surgery in the next six months to a year."

Rick continues, "I had gone through a whole series of tests. I had elevated cholesterol and blood pressure. I was forty-five pounds overweight and clinically obese." Rick and Carolyn continued to educate themselves on vegan living. "We saw the documentary *Forks over Knives,* featuring Dr. Caldwell B. Esselstyn Jr., MD, and realized we had to make a change." And their change was dramatic. "We opened up the cupboard and threw away all the oils and dairy products. Then we went shopping."

Dr. Esselstyne's diet, as outlined in *Prevent & Reverse Heart Disease,* emphasizes not just plant-based living but the elimination of oil, avocado, and nuts. The diet is plentiful in nutrient dense fruits, vegetables, legumes, and whole grains without added fats.[36]

"For the next year we both followed Dr. Esselstyne's program and never felt better in our lives. We also learned that a plant-based lifestyle could delay or prevent Alzheimer's disease, which my wife's mother, sister, and brother all died from. Today her brother is in its final stages. "

The Power of the Plant

Rick's new diet resulted in short and long term changes to his health and appearance. He recalls, "Within two months, my total cholesterol dropped seventy points. My

---

[35]Martin, David S., *From Omnivore to Vegan: The Dietary Education of Bill Clinton,* CNN, August 18, 2011, http://www.cnn.com/2011/HEALTH/08/18/bill.clinton.diet.vegan/

[36]Esselstyne, Jr., Caldwell B., *Prevent & Reverse Heart Disease: The Revolutionary, Scientifically Proven, Nutrition-Based Cure,* pp. 4-5

good cholesterol was up and the bad cholesterol was down. By the time I had my surgery ten months later, I had lost thirty-two pounds. Even the doctor mentioned how good I looked."

And Rick isn't the only one who benefitted from the new lifestyle. Today, he says that Carolyn, who has now been plant-based for four years "is still as sharp memory-wise as the day I met her thirty-five years ago. I don't know if it's because of the vegan diet, but it's hard to say that it's *not* because of it."

Balanced Diet, Balanced Life
Rick and Carolyn have every intention of keeping their plant-based lifestyle, and demonstrate a commitment to animals and the environment in many areas of their lives. "We still are and always will be 100 percent vegan. We have learned so much about the horrible suffering of farm animals and the toll that animal agriculture is doing to our planet. We donate to and volunteer at farm sanctuaries." Rick is a board member of Full Circle Farm Sanctuary, a Warm Springs, Georgia based non-profit organization that provides a safe haven for rescued farm animals. The Solans also own and operate a green certified carpet cleaning company, Prestige Chem Dry. Their lives reflect a full

commitment to a healthy life and a healthy planet.

No Energy Shortage in North Carolina
The Solans also experienced a newfound vigor that changed their lifestyle completely. "Prior to going vegan, I had never run a mile in my life. But today, I completed my first half marathon at age fifty-eight, ran the Golden Gate half marathon, and will be running my first Miami Marathon. Carolyn broke her ankle training for a triathlon, but since recovering has completed 5 and 10ks."

Summary: Rick & Carolyn Solan
Age of Change to Veganism:
Rick: 54/Carolyn: 60
Current Ages: Rick: 60/Carolyn: 67
Statistics/Changes:
- Rick has reduced his blood pressure and overall cholesterol. He lost thirty-two pounds in the first two months of

going vegan, and ran his first marathon at age fifty-eight.

- Carolyn believes the vegan lifestyle has helped her stave off Alzheimer's, a condition that has effected three of her family members. She will run her first triathlon at age sixty-five.

Original Motivator/Turning Point:

- Rick's diagnosis of a heart valve problem happened just before seeing a CNN Program on Bill Clinton's diet to reverse heart disease.
- Seeing the *Forks Over Knives* documentary and reading *Prevent & Reverse Heart Disease* by Dr. Caldwell B. Esselstyne Jr., MD.

Rick's Tip for New Vegans Over 40:

Use Google; that's what we did. There's so much information on the internet. I would spend hours at a time reading everything I could find. That's the best place to go. A lot of the information given on Facebook is not accurate.

Biggest Obstacle:

Learning to cook in a new way. Our meals were basic at first, but now it's become an adventure, getting involved with new cook books and recipes.

What Helped Ease the Transition:

We just changed our whole lifestyle. In pre-vegan days, we were couch potatoes. We worked, came home, ate, and watched TV. Today, we don't even have cable; we just have rabbit ears. We go to bed early and get up early.

Questions to Consider:

1. What, if any, health issues in your life can be reduced or eliminated through a change in diet?
2. Do you pay attention to how much oils and fats are in your diet? Can these be reduced by substituting fresh herbs or spices to add flavor?
3. What if any habits are currently not contributing to your health? (e.g., being a couch potato, watching too much TV, junk food)
4. Have you used Google to research better ways of eating, healthier recipes, or reliable sources on healthy living?
5. Which books or documentaries have had an impact on your diet or lifestyle? Which ones do you want to add to your read/watch list?

BONUS RECIPE

CAROLYN'S HUMMUS

This hummus recipe is truly special. Carolyn has omitted the olive oil, a key ingredient in traditional hummus recipes, to make it a heart-healthy treat. She has also added a kick of jalapeño peppers. Rick says it was a key recipe for him during his transition to veganism. "I ate a ton of this when we first changed. I eat it as a dip with celery and carrots, and on sandwiches as a cheese substitute. My veggie sandwiches, veggie burgers, and wraps all include hummus." Once you try it, you'll undoubtedly find many ways to incorporate it into your diet.

Ingredients

1 (15.5 oz.) can garbanzo beans (drain but reserve liquid)

2 tsps. lemon

1 tsps. cumin

2–3 tsp. Frank's Hot Sauce or Sriracha

2 cloves garlic, chopped

1 tbsp. sliced jalapeño peppers (from a jar)

1 tbsp. tahini

Directions

1. Put all ingredients in a food processor and mix for about 1 minute. If more liquid is needed, add water or the drained garbanzo bean liquid. Don't add too much liquid or your hummus will turn into soup!

2. If you like to turn up the heat, add more hot sauce.

CHAPTER 14

✦

The Beginning

*"A butterfly flapping its wings in South America can
affect the weather in Central Park."*
—Edward Lorenz

This colloquial translation of the Butterfly Theory is based on a discovery through the research of Edward Lorenz, a mathematician and meteorologist at the Massachusetts Institute of Technology. The initial concept behind this theory was that a single occurrence, no matter how seemingly inconsequential, can change the course of the world forever.[37] It is something to ponder now that you've learned small yet significant changes that can have a profound impact on your health, your life, and your planet.

If you've reached this point, you've been through the 52-week process of leaning in to veganism. You've experienced a new way of eating that feels as comfortable as the old way, while leaving you leaner and more energized. You've developed some new habits to structure your environment for success. Finally, you've been reminded of something you've known all along: that kindness, even practiced in the simplest of gestures, is sacred, healing, and transformative to you and those around you. And that kindness, like the butterfly flap, will have far-reaching effects.

Your Choices Matter

Most of all, know that if you go vegan full-time, you will save hundreds of animals each year. Even if you do it one day a week, you will still make an impact—don't feel it has to be all or nothing. Continue to honor yourself when you make kind and humane choices. Think about how those choices extend beyond the dinner plate to the people in your life. All living beings are deserving of kindness. And with your new way of eating, you are consciously practicing kindness at least three times a day (plus snacks and dessert!). Never underestimate the value of

[37] http://www.bibliotecapleyades.net/ciencia/ciencia_
climatechange25.htm

those gestures to make the world a better place, to reduce suffering of animals and the planet, and to expand your definition of love and your circle of compassion.

If you still want a simpler and even healthier way of life, I will bring your attention back to the beginning when I said that the best way to eat is to eliminate all animal products and to eliminate oil and fat (or at least reduce fats to 10 percent of your daily intake). If you want to make a vegan way of life even easier, you can simply enjoy grains, fruits, beans, and veggies, raw or steamed. For example, a plate of brown rice with black beans, and fresh salsa. Don't feel the need to always have a recipe if you are pressed for time. Choose fruit to satisfy a sweet tooth. Use fresh herbs to enhance any meal. By doing these things you will bring a new simplicity to your life, but the recipes in this book will always be here for you when you want to take the time to make healthy comfort food recipes. As you continue to evolve into new ways of eating, gravitate toward the soups and salads, and choose the recipes with vegan meats when you feel the need to have a heartier meal. On those recipes that call for sautéing vegetables in oil, you can now start to sauté with vegetable broth instead. Every step is getting you closer to

health. Default to using balsamic vinegar or rice wine vinegar on your salad with no oil when possible. Reach for fruits and veggies instead of a vending machine snack.

Finally, consider eliminating products from your life that bring harm to animals including:

- Elimination of fur coats or other fur products
- Elimination of leather, wool, or silk
- Elimination of shampoos, cleansers, or any products that are tested on animals. Many of the best quality shampoos and cleaning products are now cruelty-free and are of a much higher quality than other products on the market. Read product labels to look for the cruelty-free PETA or leaping bunny logos.

Start the Process of Making Kind Choices Every Day

Know that this is a process. Know that you have come a long way. Know that this is not something you *have* to do. You can make a conscious choice to be kind at every meal, and you can also do that with every product purchase you make. You can do it with every person as well.

The good news is, it's easier than ever to be a kind consumer. Vegan restaurants are popping up everywhere. Green products are growing in popularity. Cruelty-free clothing like imitation leather products, faux furs, and other fashions are growing in number and helping us feel beautiful inside and out.

Remember that you can experience greater happiness when your lifestyle, behaviors, and values are in alignment. If you value kindness (and I think most people are inherently kind), you have learned how to bring that into your home, your kitchen, and your body in the most basic yet profound way. You can practice it with every choice you make.

What once seemed like a mundane trip to the grocery store is now a thoughtful, conscious act. Everything we do is meaningful if we choose to give it meaning. And when we give meaning to what we used to consider ordinary daily tasks, we become fully engaged in our lives and benefit from our conscious choices. Ultimately we will experience fewer illnesses, reduced destruction of the planet (which includes animals), and an attitude of kindness which permeates everything we do—how we treat our spouse, our children, our friends, and strangers. The kindness we give will be noticed. Others will be touched by your actions and may in turn think about their own capacity for caring. Studies have shown that when you are kind to someone there is an increase in the serotonin levels in your body and theirs. Serotonin is a chemical neurotransmitter that makes us feel good—a lack of it is linked to depression. What's even more interesting is that if someone observes you being kind to another person it also increases the observer's serotonin levels simply by watching your act of kindness. Never underestimate the power of your good deeds. We can change the world through these simple, conscious practices. The daily tasks of everyday life have now become sacred because you have chosen to acknowledge them as sacred and engage in them with a newfound perspective and devotion.

A Mother's Lasting Lesson

When I was about eight years old, my mother, an incredibly kind, generous, and religious woman, shared something with me that changed me forever. In an effort to impress upon me the importance of being kind to everyone, she spoke these words from the Bible:

"Be not forgetful to entertain strangers, for thereby some have entertained angels unawares."
—Hebrews 13:2

She only said this one time and I never forgot it. It filled me with wonder. "There are angels among us and I don't know who they are?" I marveled. I went to school the next day and realized that I must be kind to everyone, just in case. What if the angel was someone in my classroom? Maybe it was the boy who greeted me with a smile when I walked through the door. Or the girl whose hands were so cold on a winter day in Pennsylvania because her parents couldn't afford to buy her mittens (I gave her mine). Or the kid with the thick glasses who was weird and introverted that no one talked to. I was kind to all of them. Which one or ones were angels? As a child, it fascinated me. As an adult, it simply became my world view. Not just because of the Bible verse, but because I witnessed my mother practicing kindness every day. It was simply who she was. My sister Susan is the same way. As I grew older, it occurred to me that everyone was an angel and had divinity within them. Everyone was and is deserving of kindness. It also occurred to me that this circle of kindness should expand to include animals. Who am I to say that animals are not angels in another form? If you look into the eyes of a puppy, a cow, a pig, or a rabbit, you will undoubtedly see the most innocent of souls. An energy. A being with a beating heart who wants to be alive just as much as you do. A being that wants to eat, sleep, frolic, and care for its offspring. Who am I to say they are not angels? Who am I to say they are not deserving of kindness? And how can I turn my head when I know what is happening to them behind the carefully guarded walls of factory farms, slaughterhouses, pharmaceutical testing laboratories, or other similar entombments? That's why this way of eating has never been about willpower (which I still don't have). It's always been about making the choice that allows me to sleep at night.

If we are truly the superior beings of our planet, does that superiority give us a right to harm animals or a responsibility to protect them just as we would a child, an elderly family member, or anyone who is weak or vulnerable? If we take the time to care about the smallest and most defenseless creatures of the earth, it stands to reason we should care about all other beings. My mother's favorite church hymn contains the line "His eye is on the sparrow, so I know he watches me." If a sparrow's life is precious, then all lives are precious. It doesn't mean vegans care more about animals than humans. It means we care about *all* life.

It takes a great capacity to care for those who can't return our love. It takes daily practice and a reverence of life to believe that animals are here for reasons that have nothing to do with us. When we care about the creatures and the people of our earth, we will naturally want to preserve our planet and its resources for all who inhabit it. By eating a plant-based diet, we can eliminate world hunger, daily pain and torture, and we can begin to live lives of peace that will create, at first, a small butterfly flap, and ultimately a tidal wave of positive energy worldwide.

Every choice we make impacts our health, our animals, and our planet. We are all made by the same creator. We are connected. We are one. Eat accordingly.

ABOUT THE AUTHORS

Photo credit: Julie Diebolt Price

Photo credit: Photography by Andy

Sandra Sellani

Sandra is a full time marketing executive and part-time blogger for *40-Year-Old Vegan* (www.40YOV.com). She is currently the Chief Marketing Officer for See Jane Go, Inc., a Southern-California based ride-hail company for women. She has an Executive MBA from Pepperdine University in Malibu, California. Sandra completed her culinary training at Matthew Kenney Culinary Academy in Los Angeles, California, and holds a certification in Plant-Based Nutrition from the T. Colin Campbell Center for Nutritional Studies. Sandra currently resides in Newport Beach, California.

Susan Sellani-Hosage, MS, SPHR, SHRM-SCP

Susan's career includes management, strategic planning, and human resources assignments with local, national, and international companies. Susan has been a member of Misericordia University's graduate faculty and has also instructed national SHRM classes through the University of Scranton's Professional Development Center. She and twin sister Sandra learned to cook at an early age from their Italian mother, grandmothers, and aunt. Susan currently resides Wyoming, Pennsylvania with her husband, Stephen.

ACKNOWLEDGMENTS

Our heartfelt gratitude goes to the many people who made this book possible

Our outstanding editor Nicole Mele and the remarkable people at Skyhorse Publishing for creating a receptive, supportive, and author-friendly environment. Your willingness to give us creative freedom and input to create a book that reflects our vision is a gift beyond measure.

Jane Velez-Mitchell, a journalistic titan, animal advocate extraordinaire, and kind, generous spirit who, without hesitation, agreed to contribute her time and beautifully crafted words to compose the foreword of this book. Jane tirelessly educates the world on animal rights and veganism. You are a constant inspiration and we are forever grateful for your contribution.

Bobby Theodore, a lifelong friend who ignited an enduring passion for vegan living.

The featured vegans who generously shared their stories: Julie Featherman, Tim Haft, Marty Krutulow, Tom Nowak, Sharon Palmer, RD, and Rick and Carolyn Solan.

Matthew Kenney and the staff of Matthew Kenney Culinary Academy in Los Angeles for their educational facilities and creative brilliance.

Julie Diebolt Price for her photographic instruction.

Our good friend Melissa Platt for her ongoing support and sage advice.

Our mother Angie Sellani, Aunt Lena Sellani, and grandmothers Elvira Sellani and Josephine Maira for more than half a century of caring, kindness, and delicious meals always made with love.

All the people who endorsed and offered praise for this project.

The 11,000+ and growing Facebook followers of the 40-Year-Old Vegan, we thank you for being part of this movement.

RESESOURCES

52-Weeks-to-Vegan: The Meal Plan

Beyond Meat Beefy Crumbles · www.beyondmeat.com
Bonne Maman Raspberry Preserves · www.bonnemaman.us
Candy Corn · www.brachs.com
Chao Vegan Cheese · www.fieldroast.com/product/chao-slices/
Earth Balance Natural Buttery Spread · www.earthbalancenatural.com
Ezekiel Bread · www.foodforlife.com
Field Roast Vegan Sausages · www.fieldroast.com
Follow Your Heart Vegan Egg · www.followyourheart.com
Gardein Meatless Products · www.gardein.com
Garden Burger Vegan Burger · www.gardenburger.com
Hampton Creek Just Mayo · www.hamptoncreek.com
Happy Cow Resource/Website · www.happycow.net
Kite Hill Vegan Cheese · www.kite-hill.com
Lightlife Vegan Bacon Strips · www.lightlife.com/products/smart-bacon
MaraNatha All Natural Almond Butter · www.maranathafoods.com
Miyoko's Kitchen Vegan Cheese · www.miyokoskitchen.com
Morning Star Farm Vegan Burgers & Breakfast Sausages · www.morningstarfarms.com
Ojio Raw Cacao Nibs · www.myojio.com
Silk Plant-Based Milks · www.silk.com
So Delicious Milk, Ice-Cream, Coco Whip · www.sodeliciousdairyfree.com
Subway Sandwiches · www.subway.com
Swedish Fish · www.swedishfish.com
Sweet and Sara Marshmallows · www.sweetandsara.com
Tofurkey Meatless Products · www.tofurkey.com
Twizzlers Licorice · www.hersheys.com
Vegenaise Vegan Spread · www.followyourheart.com
Z Pizza (Berkeley Soy Pizza) · www.zpizza.com

INDEX

CONVERSION CHARTS

METRIC AND IMPERIAL CONVERSIONS
(These conversions are rounded for convenience)

Ingredient	Cups/Tablespoons/Teaspoons	Ounces	Grams/Milliliters
Butter	1 cup = 16 tablespoons = 2 sticks	8 ounces	230 grams
Cheese, shredded	1 cup	4 ounces	110 grams
Cream cheese	1 tablespoon	0.5 ounce	14.5 grams
Cornstarch	1 tablespoon	0.3 ounce	8 grams
Flour, all-purpose	1 cup/1 tablespoon	4.5 ounces/0.3 ounce	125 grams/8 grams
Flour, whole wheat	1 cup	4 ounces	120 grams
Fruit, dried	1 cup	4 ounces	120 grams
Fruits or veggies, chopped	1 cup	5 to 7 ounces	145 to 200 grams
Fruits or veggies, puréed	1 cup	8.5 ounces	245 grams
Honey, maple syrup, or corn syrup	1 tablespoon	.75 ounce	20 grams
Liquids: cream, milk, water, or juice	1 cup	8 fluid ounces	240 milliliters
Oats	1 cup	5.5 ounces	150 grams
Salt	1 teaspoon	0.2 ounce	6 grams
Spices: cinnamon, cloves, ginger, or nutmeg (ground)	1 teaspoon	0.2 ounce	5 milliliters
Sugar, brown, firmly packed	1 cup	7 ounces	200 grams
Sugar, white	1 cup/1 tablespoon	7 ounces/0.5 ounce	200 grams/12.5 grams
Vanilla extract	1 teaspoon	0.2 ounce	4 grams

OVEN TEMPERATURES

Fahrenheit	Celsius	Gas Mark
225°	110°	$1/4$
250°	120°	$1/2$
275°	140°	1
300°	150°	2
325°	160°	3
350°	180°	4
375°	190°	5
400°	200°	6
425°	220°	7
450°	230°	8